**Something
To Think About**

DATE DUE			

Something To Think About

An Anthology of Stories, Poems and Songs
from the BBC Radio Series
Edited by Paddy Bechely
Illustrated by Alan Burton

British Broadcasting Corporation

This book is set in Linotron
Century Schoolbook 11/13 point
© The British Broadcasting Corporation
and the Contributors 1982
First published 1982
Reprinted 1984, 1985, 1988
Published at the request
of the Educational Broadcasting Council
for the United Kingdom
by BBC Books,
a division of BBC Enterprises Limited,
Woodlands, 80 Wood Lane,
London W12 0TT.
Printed in England by Yale Press, London
ISBN 0 563 31975 5

Contents

Making Friends

Do you have a special friend?
How do you make a new friend?
Have you ever played with someone who was lonely?

A New Friend

'What's your most favourite time of the day?' said Michael to
Mark, his friend. 'I mean, your most favourite, favourite time.'
'Bed time,' said Mark. 'Then I can curl up in bed with my cuddly
hippopotamus.'
'No, no, silly,' said Michael. 'I mean your most favourite, favourite,
favourite time at school.'
'That's the silliest queston I ever heard,' said Mark. 'The answer's
playtime of course.'
And it so happened that just at that moment the bell went, and it
was playtime!

Ding a ling a ling a ling a ling!

Michael and Mark are best friends. They always play together. In
fact Michael likes playing with Mark so much he never plays with
anyone else. Their favourite game is buses.

Brrm, brr brrr brrr brrrrm brr brrr brrrrm they go!

One day, when Mark was being the driver, this is what happened.
'All aboard, hold tight, move along the bus, tickets please, *ding
ding*,' said Mark. Michael got on.

To get on a bus – when you're playing buses – you stand behind the
driver and hold tight to his pullover. Then you go *brrr brrr brrrrm*
all round the playground.

'Where do you want go?' said Mark to Michael.
'To the zoo please, driver!' said Michael to Mark.
'The zoo? That's ten pence. All aboard, hold tight, *ding a ling*, off
we go.' And off they went.

It was then that Mark heard another boy calling to them.
'Michael, Mark!' shouted the other boy, whose name was David.
'Can I play?'

Mark was going *brrm brrm* like a bus so loudly he didn't hear him
at first.
8

'Michael! Mark!' The other boy shouted more loudly than ever.
'Who's calling us?' said Mark.
'Um, er, um, er . . . That's David' said Michael. 'We don't want to play with him. Come on bus, keep going.'
But David didn't stop calling to them. 'Please, Michael. Please Mark. Can I play on your bus?'
Michael really didn't want David to play because he liked playing with Mark all on his own. So he said 'No, sorry David. This game's just for two. Keep going bus, *brrrm brrrm. Brrm brrrm brrrm.*'
And off they went.
And David had to go on playing all on his own.

Poor old David.

A few days later, it was poor old Mark. He was playing buses, again. With Michael, again. And he didn't feel very well. 'I think I've got a cold coming,' he said.

Mark couldn't come to school at all next day. His mummy told the teacher, 'I'm awfully sorry, but Mark will have to stay home for a week.' 'Oh dear,' said the teacher, 'is it a bad cold?'
'No,' said Mark's mummy. 'It's mumps.'

'Mark can't come to school for a whole week,' Michael told his mummy. 'He's got lumps.'
'Mumps, dear,' said his mummy. 'You'll have to find someone else to play with.'
'But I don't want to play with anyone's else, Mum,' said Michael.
'I like playing with Mark.'
'Well you'll have to play on your own for a week, then, won't you?' said his Mum.

So, at playtime next day, Michael tried playing buses on his own.
'*Ding a ling,*' he said miserably. 'All aboard. Hold tight. Tickets please. Oh dear.'
It wasn't much fun playing on his own.

He tried a really good, really fast game of trains. He really raced round the playground. But that wasn't much fun either.
He tried aeroplanes. He tried ships. And he tried being Tarzan.
But no one said, 'Cor, what a super game,' or anything like that.
So he got fed up. Because it really wasn't any fun at all, playing on his own. Now he knew how David had felt, the week before, when he was on his own, and he hadn't let him play.

9

'*Brrm brrrm*' he said, and drove his bus over to a corner of the playground. He was a very sad little bus indeed.
When all of a sudden, he heard . . .

'*Brrrm brrrm, brrrm brrrrm.*' It was another bus.

'All aboard, tickets please, hold tight, mind your heads, plenty of room upstairs and *ding a ling a ling a ling.*'
This really did look like fun.

The new bus was David.

'Hey driver, driver, David,' shouted Michael, jumping up and feeling a lot less sad than he had been. 'Driver!'
'Yes?'
'Is your bus going to the zoo?'
'Yes, hop in,' said David.
And Michael and David played together all that playtime. They both enjoyed it much more than playing on their own.

All that week, while Mark was ill, they played games together. Monday, it was buses, and going to the zoo. Tuesday was trains. On Wednesday they were police drivers chasing robbers in a car. And on Thursday they went to the moon in a spaceship. When they got to the moon, they sat on pretend spacehoppers, and used these to jump over mountains as lightly as feathers, and they found a magic jungle with animals in it, and they brought twenty-four of these back, to go in the zoo, which they were planning to visit once again, in the bus, at playtime on Friday.
Except that on Friday David was a little bit sad.

'Mark comes back next week,' he said, 'Then I won't have anyone to play with again.'
'Well I know what,' said Michael, 'I'll ask Mark if you can play with us.'

On Monday Mark came back. His lumps (I mean his mumps) were gone. As soon as the bell went for playtime, he was so excited he ran straight out into the playground and started up his bus. 'My turn to be driver,' he shouted. 'I've been ill for a week. All aboard, tickets please, hold tight, *ding ding.*'
'Are you going to the zoo?' shouted Michael
'Yes, all aboard.'
But Michael didn't just start playing with Mark, not just like that, because he had something to ask him first.
10

'Mark,' said Michael.

'What is it?'

'Can David come too?' said Michael. 'You see, David and I played together all last week while you were ill and he'll be lonely if he plays on his own again.'

'Of course he can play,' said Mark.

'You mean you don't mind?'

'No. I don't mind,' said Mark. 'But I'll tell you what. We'll have to think up games for three now.'

'Oh yes, so we will,' said Michael. 'Well, for a start we can get three on a bus!'

'*All aboard, ding a ling, hold tight!*'

Now nobody's playing on their own!

Colin Davis

It's Not Much Fun

It's not much fun when you're playing on your own
No, it's not much fun if you're playing all alone.
You can race yourself and chase yourself,
                and drive yourself around,
You can hide yourself and slide yourself
                and push you to the ground,
You can tell yourself a story, a poem or a song,
But it's not much fun to have to play
                on your own for long.

It's not much fun when you're playing on your own
No, it's not much fun if you're playing all alone.
You can catch the bus you drive yourself
                and take you to the zoo,
You can take the train or aeroplane
                and be policeman too,
You can put yourself in handcuffs and turn your sirens on
But it's not much fun to have to play
                on your own for long.

Colin Davis

Mother Crin

Once upon a time, in the West Indies, three brothers lived with their mother in a little house at the edge of a field in which sugar-cane grew.

It was that 'once-upon-a-time' time when people believed in witches, and were frightened of them. There were plenty of witches in the islands of the West Indies, and ghosts too, which the people called jumbies. But this story is about a witch. Her name was Old Mother Crin.

The three brothers and their mother were quite poor. To get the money they needed to live they kept chickens and sold the eggs to the shop in the nearby village. To get to the village they had to walk along a path that went through the field of sugar-cane. The three boys took turns to take the eggs to the shop. On the first day of this story it was Reuben's turn. He was the eldest brother.

'Reuben!' said his mother. 'Here are the eggs for the shop. Go carefully, now, and make sure that you bring the money back safe.'

Reuben was standing on the doorstep looking out at the sugar-cane, which was waving in the breeze and rustling like knives being sharpened. Reuben was a shy and fearful boy, and he was thinking that he would much rather *not* do the job that day.

'At this time of year that cane is so tall,' he thought to himself. 'Something could hide in there and jump out at me. Maybe a giant rat.' And he shuddered.
'Hurry up,' said his mother.
'O.K. Ma', said Reuben. And he took the basket of eggs and set off along the path. After just a few yards he was out of sight of the house and amongst the cane. It grew taller than his head in a tangle of stalks and long, sharp leaves.

'This canefield is so big,' he thought, in his fearful way, 'that it could hide other things besides rats.
12

A witch or a jumbie ghost could be living in there.'

Just as he thought that, he heard a voice.
'Reuben!' it croaked.
Reuben jumped.
'Who's that?' he said.
'Reuben!' croaked the voice again.
Reuben looked around him but he could see nothing.
'Here I am, boy,' said the voice. 'In the cane by the side of the path.'
Reuben looked into the cane and saw a heap of black rags lying on
the ground.

'Who are you?' he asked in a voice that was trembling with fear.
'I'm Old Mother Crin,' said the voice, and it began to chant
'I'm Old Mother Crin
With a face like a door
That the wind pushed in.
I'm a bundle of bones
And a rattle of rags,
Give me a kind word!'

Reuben didn't wait to hear her last words. He screamed and ran.
The basket of eggs fell from his arm and the yellow yolks spilled
over the ground.
When he returned to the house, his mother scolded him for being
so frightened.
'You are a weak, fearful boy,' she said. 'You take fright at
everything. You think you hear voices and you run. I've told you
before, you must be brave.'

The second son in the family was called Jacob, and the youngest
son was called Benjamin. The next day it was Jacob's turn to take
the eggs to the shop. Jacob did not suffer from fear like Reuben,
but he was boastful, proud and violent. He armed himself with a
stick before he set off.
'You be careful, Jacob,' called his mother. 'I want those eggs safely
in the shop, and I want the money safely back here.'
'Nobody's going to frighten me,' shouted Jacob.
'And if they try, they'll wish they hadn't, because I've got a stick.'
And he slashed his stick through the air a few times as he spoke.
'Go easy, boy,' said his mother. 'Don't look for trouble.'
Jacob turned the corner of the path and disappeared out of sight
into the canefield.

'If anyone tries to frighten me, they'll wish they hadn't,' he said in a loud voice, as he marched along. 'I've never been frightened in my life. Not like Reuben. Reuben frightens easy. Not like Benjamin. Benjamin's a baby. No sir, Jacob's not the sort of person to get any sort of fright.'

Just as he said that, there was a voice at his elbow.
'Ja-cob!' it croaked.
Jacob stopped. 'Who's that?' he cried, swinging his stick.
'It's me, Jacob,' croaked the voice.
Jacob turned. 'And who are you?' he demanded, in a menacing voice. 'Speak up, or else . . .' And he swung his stick backwards and forwards.
'I'm Old Mother Crin,' said the voice, and it began to chant
'I'm Old Mother Crin
With a face like a door
That the wind pushed in.
I'm a bundle of bones
And a rattle of rags,
Give me a kind word!'

'I see you,' shouted Jacob. 'You're under that heap of old clothes over there. I'll teach you to frighten me!'
He rushed into the cane with his stick and used it wildly.
But the stick went right through the rags as if there was nothing there. Jacob hit out again. Again the stick met nothing but air.
Jacob stopped, and the stick dropped from his hand.
Then, just like Reuben, he screamed and ran. The basket of eggs fell from his arm and the yellow yolks spilled over the ground.
When he returned to the house, his mother spent even longer scolding him than she had Reuben.
'You are a rough and violent boy,' she said. 'You make trouble for everyone with your fighting ways. It's not enough to be brave. You must also be good.'

'It's my turn to take the eggs tomorrow,' said Benjamin, the youngest son.
'Don't do it,' said Reuben. 'You'll be too frightened.'
'Don't do it,' said Jacob. 'You're not strong enough.'
'Well,' said Benjamin. 'It's my turn. Do you want to do it for me, Jacob?'
Jacob didn't answer.

'Do you want to do it for me, Reuben?' asked Benjamin. Reuben didn't answer. 'Then,' said Benjamin calmly, 'I will go.'

'Good luck Benjamin,' said his mother, as she gave him the eggs next morning. But his brothers had decided to make fun of him. 'Maybe the witch won't come after Benjamin after all,' said Reuben. 'He's such a baby she might not notice him.'

'He's such a baby, he might not notice her,' said Jacob, laughing in an unpleasant sort of way.

'Have you boys got anything to laugh about?' demanded their mother. 'Get off and do some useful work.'

Benjamin set off down the path with the basket of eggs on his arm. His brothers' remarks had not worried him. He knew he was small, but he was unafraid. It was a lovely day. The sky was blue above the waving fronds of the cane. He didn't even think about the witch. But just as he passed the bend in the path his name was called.

'Benjamin!'

Benjamin stopped.

'Who's that?' he asked.

'I'm Old Mother Crin', croaked the voice.

'Oh', said Benjamin. 'Are you that Old Mother Crin my brothers saw?' He looked in the direction of the voice but he could see nothing. 'Where are you?' he said.

The voice began to chant.

'I'm Old Mother Crin
With a face like a door
That the wind pushed in . . .

'Stop, stop', said Benjamin. 'Is that you in those rags over there?'

'I'm a bundle of bones
And a rattle of rags . . .' continued the voice.

'That's true,' said Benjamin, peering at the witch where she lay in her black clothes on the ground. 'What happened to you?'

'Give me a kind word,' screeched the witch, coming to the end of her chant.

'Give you a kind word?' repeated Benjamin.

'Well . . .'. He almost couldn't think of anything to say.

'Well', he said again. 'Good morning Mistress Crin.'

'Is that kind enough?' he asked anxiously, going closer.

'It will do,' said the witch.

Benjamin looked at her. She was like a skeleton.

Her face and hands were all bones, with no skin. 'So you are Old

Mother Crin,' he said.

'Not so old,' said the witch.

Benjamin looked at her again. Something seemed to be happening to her.

'You are changing in front of my eyes,' he said.

'Right in front of your eyes,' said the witch.

'But how?' asked Benjamin, in amazement.

'You made me change,' said the witch.

'Not *me*,' said Benjamin. 'I'm just a boy. It can't be anything to do with me.'

'Yes it is,' said the witch. 'You spoke to me in a kind way. You didn't run away and you didn't try to hit me with a stick. Every minute that you talk to me I change for the better. Listen to my voice!'

'Your voice is much better,' said Benjamin. 'Not so croaky.'

'Look at my clothes,' said the witch.

Benjamin looked. All her horrible black rags were coming together into one piece, and they were changing colour from black to gold.

'Look at my face,' commanded the witch. Benjamin looked. Where there had been bare bones before there was now a real face, with beautiful black skin and shining eyes.

'See how tall I am,' she said, as she stood up straight. Benjamin was amazed. Standing before him was a tall young woman in a golden dress. Her hair was plaited and woven with beads and ribbons into a shape like a crown.

'You see,' said the woman. 'I'm not Old Mother Crin at all. I'm an African princess. I had a spell put on me in Africa over three hundred years ago. I've been waiting three hundred years for somebody to speak to me kindly. I've been forced to stay here. But now I can go. You've freed me, Benjamin. And freed everyone else too. Old Mother Crin will never frighten anyone any more. This is the end of Old Mother Crin!'

As she said the last words there was a sudden loud noise, like a clap of thunder. It made Benjamin blink, and when he opened his eyes again, she was gone.

There was nothing left of Old Mother Crin, and nothing to show where she had been. The canefield was silent. Benjamin felt dazed. He wondered whether he should go back to tell the others what had happened but he decided that they would probably say that he had been dreaming. He looked at the basket of eggs. At least

16

nothing had happened to them. With a sigh he continued on his way to the village.

When he returned to the house his mother was on the doorstep waiting for him.
'What a time you've been, Benjy,' she said. 'Did you get to the shop?'
'I did, Ma,' said Benjamin.
'Did you see the witch?' demanded Reuben.
'I did,' said Benjamin. 'Except that she wasn't a witch. She was an African princess.'
Jacob roared with laughter. 'Trust Benjamin to get it wrong,' he shouted.
'Silence, boys,' said their mother. 'Sit down, Benjamin, and tell us what happened.'
'She called my name,' said Benjamin, 'and she asked me to say a kind word. So I said 'Good morning, Mistress Crin'. And when I spoke to her she began to change. She changed right in front of my eyes. Then she said she was an African princess. Then there was a loud noise and she disappeared.'
'But weren't you frightened?' squealed Reuben.
'Weren't you angry?' yelled Jacob.
'No,' said their mother, 'Benjamin wasn't frightened. And he wasn't angry. That's how he managed to do something that you both failed to do. Benjamin was brave and good. He was brave because he didn't run away when he first saw the witch. He was good because he said a kind word to her when she asked. Being brave and good is the way to deal with witches – and with other bad things too.'
Meg Sheffield

Hello's a Handy Word

Hello's a handy word to say,
At least a hundred times a day,
Without hello what would I do
Whenever I bumped into you?
Without hello where would you be
Whenever you bumped into me?
Hello's a handy word to know
Hello, hello, hello!
Mary Ann Hoberman

18

Talking

Talk to me I want to hear your voice
Talk to me, I want to know
Who you are and what you're thinking of
Talk to me, talk to me, talk to me.

Who can hear me talking when
There's such a lot of noise?
Shopping in the supermarket
Who could hear my voice?
Walking all the way to school
The busy traffic roared
Making it impossible
To hear a single word.

Who can hear the birdsong when
The wind blows in the trees?
Who can hear the fishes talk in
Angry lashing seas?
When I talk at night the
Television drowns my words.
Sometimes it just seems to me that
No-one can be heard.

Talk to me I want to hear your voice
Talk to me I want to know
Who you are and what you're thinking of
Talk to me, talk to me, talk to me.

Talking in the playground I
Will tell you, if I may,
What my hamster had for tea
And where I like to play,
How I spend my money, and if
You will talk to me,
We can share our thinking
Talking secrets, secretly.

Sarah McNeill

The Wall

Paul, Andy and Rachel went to live in a New Town. The houses and shops and roads were all new, but every day on their way to school, they had to walk along a winding lane, past some old houses that once had been part of a nearby village.

At the end of the lane was a high stone wall, and the children had to walk beside this wall in single file because the pavement was so narrow. Set back into the wall, about halfway along, was a large wooden gate that was always shut. It had peeling paint and there were children's names scribbled in chalk all over it. In the corners of the gateway the wind had blown piles of rubbish and dust, old sweet papers and crisp packets, but it was a good place for Paul, Andy and Rachel to meet their friends because they could step back there out of the way of the big lorries that roared up the lane on their way to the motorway.

'There's a house behind this wall,' Rachel told her brothers. 'An old woman lives there but she never comes out.'
'You can see the upstairs windows from across the road,' said Paul. 'I've seen her looking out. She watches us, you know.'
'Perhaps she's a witch!' said Andy.

Then one morning, as the children were passing the gate, it opened suddenly – and there she was! She was tall and thin and very angry.
'Here, you three!' she called. 'I want to speak to you.'
'Do you mean us?' said Rachel.
'Of course I mean you!' said the old woman crossly.
'We'll be late for school,' said Rachel, but the old woman grabbed hold of her arm. Then they both stepped back quickly into the gateway as a big lorry swung by close to the path.

'Juggernauts!' said the old woman. 'Big, ugly, noisy, dangerous things. I hate them. It never used to be like this before the New Town came and the new road. It used to be peaceful here.'
'Well, it's not our fault!' said Paul.

20

'*This* is your fault,' said the old woman, pointing to the rubbish by the gate. 'This has only happened since your new school opened. You hang about outside here every day, leaving all your mess – look at it – ice-cream papers, cartons, bits of comics –'

'But you can't blame us for all this,' said Paul. 'We've only just come here.'

'I've seen you!' exclaimed the old lady. 'You're up and down here twice a day. I've been watching you. And look at all this scribbling on my gate! Well, I'm not having it, do you hear? I want your names and addresses and I shall go straight to your teacher and your parents as well.'

'But we haven't done anything!' cried Paul. 'Honest we haven't.'

Rachel pulled her arm free and began to run.

'Come back!' shouted the old woman. 'Do you hear? Come back!'

But the children were running away up the lane. At the crossroads they stopped to get their breath.

'Do you think she'll find out where we live?' asked Rachel.

"Course not!' said Paul.

'She'll come up to the school,' said Andy.

'You're scared!' said Paul.

'No I'm not,' said Andy. 'But she's not fair. *We* didn't drop that rubbish.'

'I did drop a crisp packet there last night,' said Rachel.

'Well, we didn't drop it *all*,' said Andy. 'She's horrible. I'm going to write Mouldy Meadows all over her gate.'

'Yes! Mouldy Meadows. That's her name, Mrs. Meadows,' said Paul. 'We'll write MOULDY MEADOWS in red chalk all over her gate.'

'Great!' said Andy. 'In big letters.'

After school, Paul and Andy brought some red chalk and did just what they said they would do. Mrs. Meadows was looking out of one of her top windows. Rachel, who was watching from the other side of the road could see that she looked very angry. She banged on the glass, and then her face disappeared.

'Hurry up!' called Rachel to the boys. 'She's coming after you.'

They ran away, but nothing happened. The gate didn't open.

'She *will* come up to the school now,' said Andy.

But he was wrong. Their names weren't called out at assembly and they didn't see anything of Mrs. Meadows for several days. A week passed. It rained, and the red chalk was washed off the gate.

Then one morning as they passed the wall, they saw that the gate was open. Rachel began to run. Suddenly there was a screech of brakes, and a big lorry swerved on to the pavement in front of her. Paul grabbed her and pulled her close to the wall. The lorry bumped down off the kerb and drove me away up the lane.

'We could have been killed!' said Andy. 'Why did he swerve like that?'

'Perhaps a dog ran across the road in front of him,' said Paul.

Then they saw something at the foot of the wall. A small tabby cat was lying in a heap as if someone had thrown it away. Rachel knelt down beside it.

'One of the wheels must have hit it,' she said.

The cat made a faint mewing sound and lifted its head.

'It's alive,' said Andy. 'Look, it's trying to get up. It can't be hurt very badly.'

'We can't leave it here,' said Rachel. 'It might wander out on to the road again. Let's take it inside the gate.'

Andy stared at her. 'You mean – take it into Mouldy Meadows' garden?' he said.

'Yes,' said Rachel. 'Away from all the traffic.'

Gently she lifted the cat. They carried it through the gate and put it down in some long grass under an apple tree. The cat was purring now, and began to lick one of its paws.

'Look out!' cried Paul. Rachel glanced up, towards the house. Mrs. Meadows was running along the path. But she wasn't taking any notice of the children. She was looking only at the cat, and calling out as she ran –

'Tiger! Oh, my poor little Tiger! What have they done to you?'

The cat ran to her, mewing, and she picked it up and held it close to her face.

'We think a lorry must have hit him,' said Rachel. 'He was lying on the path against the wall, so we brought him in here.'

'Someone must have left the gate open,' said Mrs. Meadows.

'We didn't know he was your cat,' said Paul. 'Will he be all right?'

'Yes I think so,' said Mrs. Meadows, and she smiled at him.

Andy was staring towards the house. 'Are they your cats too?' he cried in astonishment.

Out of the back door of the house, and along the path and across the grass cats were running towards the old woman, calling with strange small cries. There were young cats and old cats, black cats and grey cats, and one of the purest white. They rubbed themselves against the children's legs.

'Are they really all yours?' asked Rachel.

'I suppose they are,' said Mrs. Meadows. 'They're lost cats, and no-one ever seems to come to claim them, even though I do put cards in the post office window, so I suppose I'm stuck with them. I suppose it's all you lot coming here, people changing houses, and all this coming and going. Cats don't like change. People bring lost cats to me now when they find them wandering.'

'How many have you got?' asked Paul.

'I've almost lost count,' said Mrs. Meadows, 'eleven I think. No, there are three more kittens in the kitchen. Goodness knows what I'm going to do with them while I'm away. I've been poorly for two weeks, and the doctor says I must go to hospital. But what will happen to this lot I just don't know.'

'Couldn't you take them to a cattery?' asked Paul.

'I couldn't afford it on my pension,' said Mrs. Meadows. 'Besides, they'll be better if they stay here.'

'Couldn't you ask someone to come in and feed them while you're away?' suggested Rachel.

'Yes, but who?' said Mrs. Meadows. 'I don't go out much and I don't know all the new people round here. Anyway, thanks for bringing Tiger home.' She turned away. 'Mind you shut that gate now.'

'If you like,' said Rachel, 'we could make sure it's shut every time we go by. Would that help?'

'Well, it would be something,' said Mrs. Meadows.

Andy bent down and stroked one of the cats, and almost under his breath said, 'I'm sorry about that red chalk on your gate.'

'I'm glad to hear it,' said Mrs. Meadows, 'and now off you go. I've got fourteen breakfasts to start thinking about.'

Andy stood up and looked at Paul, and then at Rachel, and they both nodded as if they knew what he was thinking.

'Would you like us to come in every day and feed the cats?' he said.

'You?' said Mrs. Meadows.

'We promise we wouldn't forget,' said Rachel quickly. 'We could come every day after school and you could leave enough tins for them and open that little greenhouse place over there for them all to sleep in.'

'And we could bring some milk for them each day,' said Paul. 'Oh please – please let us.'

'Well,' said Mrs. Meadows, 'it would only be for ten days. But you must ask your parents first.'

'Yes, we'll ask them tonight,' said Andy. 'And we'll come back and tell you tomorrow. We'll be able to see how Tiger is, too.'

So that is what they did. While Mrs. Meadows was in hospital, the children fed the cats and checked every day that the door in the wall was always safely shut. They swept up all the rubbish round the gate, too, so that when Mrs. Meadows came home again it was all clean and tidy.

Andy and Paul thought it very strange that Mrs. Meadows seemed to change so quickly, but Rachel said she wasn't surprised at all. As she said, it's sometimes very hard to get to know what a person is really like when they live behind a high stone wall.

Kay McManus

When Things Go Wrong

Do you sometimes have a day when everything seems to go wrong?   Have you ever felt a bad temper getting worse and worse inside you?

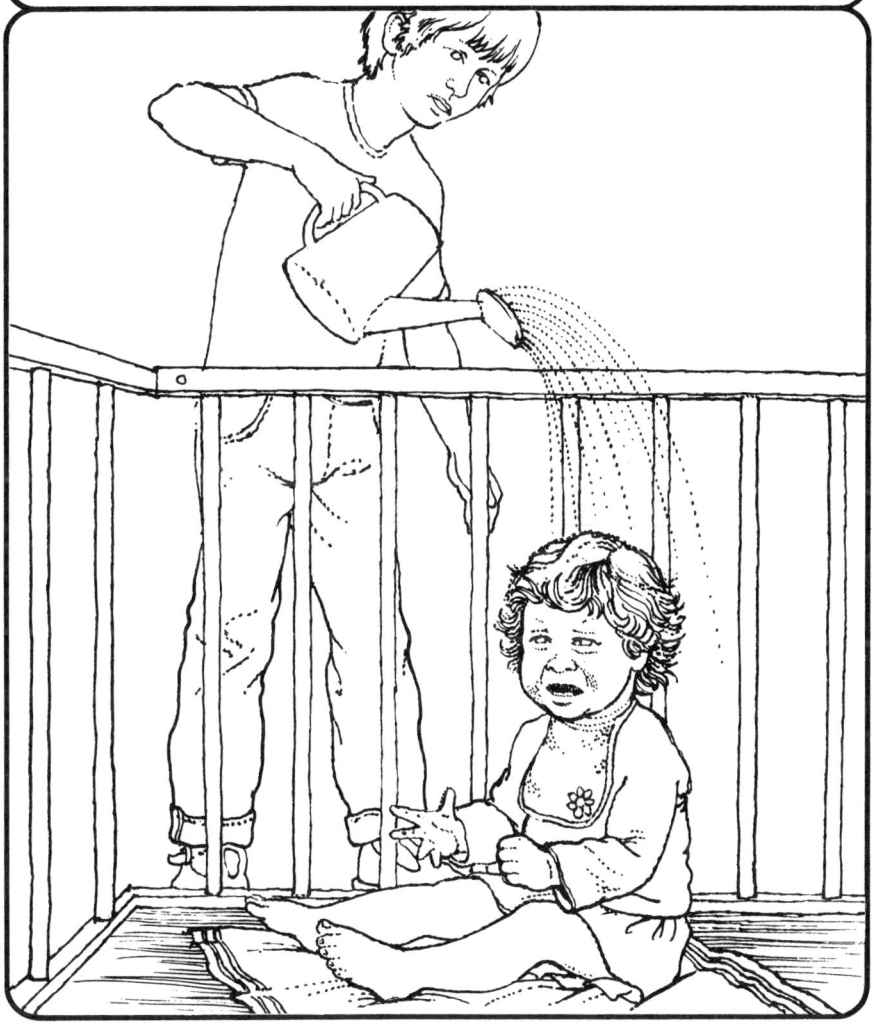

There's Another Day Tomorrow

Once upon a time there was a boy called Michael. He lived with his Mum, and his baby sister Susie, and his Dad, who was out at work all day. Dad was a long distance lorry driver.

Michael liked to play outside in the garden, with Bouncer the dog. He was happy most of the time. But now and again Michael had a bad day, when things went wrong, and got blacker and blacker. Then inside himself he got angrier and angrier. The hot black anger wouldn't stop.

But this story begins on one of his good days. It was Michael's birthday, and he woke up feeling happy: 'It's Friday. It's my birthday. It's a special day today.'
Michael was pleased with his birthday presents. From Mum he had a round, green paddling pool; from Susie, a yellow plastic watering can; from Auntie Mary, a picture book; from Uncle Bob, a shiny golden trumpet. His Grandma had sent him a blackboard and easel, and a box of coloured chalks for drawing pictures on the blackboard. Bouncer gave him a big yellow duster for wiping the blackboard clean again. The very best present was a bicycle, from Dad. But Dad wasn't there to help him ride it!

Mum said, 'It's no use grumbling, Michael. Your Dad has got to work. But it's Saturday tomorrow. Dad will be home all day tomorrow.'
'And he'll help me ride my bike,' said Michael.
Mum said, 'After he's mended the fence! Don't you go pestering your Dad tomorrow, or he'll never mend that fence at the bottom of the garden. Then it'll fall on that special, Super Star rose bush that Grandma gave me. And what would Grandma say?'

Michael played with his other presents all day. He was fast asleep in bed by the time his Dad got home. But as soon as he woke next morning he remembered: 'It's Saturday. Dad's home. He'll help me ride my bike. It's going to be a good, extra special day today.'

In the garden, after breakfast, Dad looked at Michael's presents. He said, 'Well, aren't you the lucky one, Michael! *I've* got to go and mend that wobbly bit of fence, before it falls over and breaks that precious rose bush.'

Dad went down to the bottom of the garden, to mend the fence with his hammer and some nails. Mum carried Susie out into the garden, and put her in her play pen on the grass. 'Now both of you be good,' she said. 'I've things to do indoors.'

Michael took the yellow plastic watering can, and filled it with water from the paddling pool. First, he watered a marigold flower. Then he watered a pansy plant. Then he went to Susie's play pen. And . . . he watered Susie! Trickles of water fell on her head, and ran down her face, and dripped on her bib. Susie screwed her eyes up, and opened her mouth, and wailed and wailed and wailed, till Mum came running out.

'Michael', she scolded. 'What a silly thing to do! Why did you do such a stupid, naughty thing? There there, Susie love, its all right!' And she picked up baby Susie and carried her indoors.

Michael's day was not such a good one any more. But he smiled when Bouncer came trotting up the garden.

'Here, Bouncer. Sit. Sit down and look at this. It's the shiny golden trumpet Uncle Bob gave me. Shall I play you a tune on my trumpet, Bouncer?'

Michael blew the trumpet, but it didn't make a tune. The noise that came out was a screeching, scraping sound. Bouncer put his nose up, and howled and howled and howled.

Dad looked up from his mending of the fence. He thought it was funny. He was laughing. But then Mrs Macintosh, the next door lady, looked over the hedge, and *she* wasn't laughing. She was frowning, and she said, 'I don't like complaining. But please could we have less noise. It's quite dreadful.'

Dad said, 'I'm sorry, Mrs Macintosh. I'm sorry.'

And he came up the garden and took away the trumpet. He said, 'Find something quiet to do, for goodness sake.'

Michael's special day was getting blacker by the minute. He patted Bouncer's head: 'I know what we'll do. We'll look at the picture book Auntie Mary gave me. Sit, Bouncer. Now, look at that. That's a great big lorry, like the one Dad drives.'

Bouncer didn't want to look. He lifted up his head, and snapped at a buzzing bumble bee.

Michael shouted, 'Look, I said, Bouncer. Look!' And he pushed the little dog's head down roughly, on the picture book, Bouncer yelped. Then he barked and barked and barked.

Mum called out of the kitchen window: 'Michael! Stop it! Oh my goodness! Can't you do anything right today? Dinner's nearly ready. Come and wash your hands.'

After dinner, they all had a sleep. Then Dad sighed, and went down the garden to mend the fence again. Mum said, 'Michael, do something sensible. Go out and draw on your blackboard or something.'

Michael went out and began to draw a lorry. But the wheels went wrong. Stupid old lorry! 'Stupid, stupid old lorry!' he shouted. And he threw the coloured chalks at the blackboard.

Dad came up the garden, and he shook his head at Michael. 'It's no use throwing things. Wipe the blackboard clean, with the big yellow duster, and make a new start. Anyway, I've finished the fence, thank goodness. So let's have a go on your bicycle, eh? Come along. Up you get. Feet on the pedals.'

Michael was pleased and smiling again. Dad said, 'Ride down the grass, slowly. I'll walk beside you. Not too fast.'

Michael rode to the bottom of the garden, where Dad had mended the fence. He felt happy. He turned around and pedalled back, slowly, to the house.

Then Dad said, 'Now Michael, ride down again. This time, go by yourself. Not too fast. Look, here's Mum coming out to watch you. Remember, Michael, you mustn't go too fast, or your feet will lose the pedals. And then you'll fall off.'

Michael rode slowly and properly at first. But it felt so good that he went a little faster. And then still faster, pushing down the pedals!

Dad called, 'Michael! I told you. Not so fast!'

And Mum shouted, 'Michael! Stop him, Dad!'

But nobody could stop him now. The pedals spun around. His feet couldn't find them. On he sped, to the bottom of the garden. And he couldn't stop. Crash! through the flower bed went the bicycle and Michael. And crash, bang! into Dad's mended fence.

Dad came and picked him up. He picked up the bicycle. His face was red and angry: 'I told you. I told you. Look what you've done now. The fence is falling over. Now I'll have to mend it all over again.'

Inside himself, Michael felt blacker and blacker, angrier and angrier. The anger wouldn't stop. It was all the bike's fault. That stupid, stupid bike! He picked up the bicycle, and threw it, hard, into the special, Super Star rose bush.

He didn't remember what happened after that, until he knew he was crying, in bed. Of course, Dad had sent him to bed. And now he was crying. Things were worse than ever, blacker than ever, but with misery now. Nobody would like him now, and nobody would care, and nothing would ever be happy any more.

It was supper time when Dad came into the bedroom, carrying some sandwiches for Michael. He sat on the bed, and Michael whispered, 'Dad, I'm sorry. Is the fence all right?'
Dad shook his head. 'No! It isn't. And the rose bush is smashed to bits. Your Mum was nearly crying.'
Michael closed his eyes, and turned away from Dad. But he heard Dad saying, 'There's another day tomorrow. Things won't seem so black tomorrow. And perhaps you can draw a better lorry tomorrow. You wiped the bad one clean. Remember? With the big yellow duster, to make a new start! And a good night's sleep is a sort of yellow duster, to wipe away the badness for a new start tomorrow. Then you can help me mend the fence, and say sorry to your Mum. And perhaps we can tell her that we'll buy her another Super Star rose bush.'
Michael turned around towards Dad, and nodded. Then he slept, to get ready for a good new beginning.

Anita Hewett

Anger

I was angry and mad,
And it seemed there was hot water inside me,
And as I got madder and madder,
The water got hotter and hotter all the time,
I was in a rage,
Then I began to see colours,
Like black and red,
Then I got madder and madder,
My eyes began to pop out of my head,
They were popping up and down,
It was horrible,
And it would not stop,
I was steaming with anger,
Nobody could stop me,
My mother could not stop me,
Then it was gone,
And I was all right,
Horrible, black madness.

Yvonne Lowe, aged 8

New Things To Do

New things to do,
New places to go
New things to learn
New people to know,
New songs to sing,
New games to play,
We'll try not to spoil
This happy new day.

New things to do,
New places to go.
New things to learn,
New people to know,
New things to see
New things to hear,
We'll try not to spoil
This happy new year.

Anita Hewett

It Wasn't My Fault

Once upon a time there were two brown birds, Mother Bird
and Father Bird, who lived in a jungle.
Other creatures lived there too, among the tall green trees.
There was Monkey, who climbed up high in the branches; Rat,
with his sharp white biting teeth; Giraffe, with his long neck;
and big grey Elephant. Elephant, the biggest of them all!

One day in early springtime the two brown birds said, 'Now!
It's time to build a good strong nest, and then to lay some eggs.
And out of the eggs will come some tiny baby birds.'

The two brown birds found a place to build their nest in the middle
of a tall, strong tree. It was not too high, not too low, and fresh
green leaves above it would shelter the nest from the burning
jungle sun.

Then day after day they flew around the jungle, collecting twigs
and roots and moss and mud to build their nest. When it was
finished Mother Bird laid speckled eggs – one, two, three, four.
She said, 'Just imagine, before very long we'll have four baby birds.'
And Father Brown Bird said, 'The eggs are safe up here.'
But Monkey, who climbed up high in the branches, was sitting on
a branch above the nest. Monkey had a paw full of hard brown
nuts. He was cracking the nuts with his teeth, and eating them.
The two brown birds said, 'Please be careful. Don't drop a nut on
our four little eggs.'
But Monkey was careless. He did drop a nut. It fell on the nest,
and smash! It broke one of the eggs.

Monkey went away through the jungle, and he said, 'It wasn't *my*
fault. Too bad! They ought to have built their nest lower down.'
The two brown birds drooped their heads, and they said, 'Now,
we shall only have three baby birds.'

Rat, with his sharp white biting teeth, came running to the trunk
of the tree and started biting it. The two brown birds said, 'Please
don't bite our tree trunk. We want it to stand up straight and strong.

There are thunderclouds coming, carrying a storm. If the storm
breaks out and the wind begins to blow, our tree will bend
from side to side and toss our nest about.'
But Rat went on biting and biting and biting, till the trunk of the
tree wasn't strong any more. Then the thunderclouds broke, and
the wind began to blow. It bent the tree from side to side and tossed
the nest about.
And one little egg fell out and broke to bits.
Rat went away through the jungle and he said, 'It wasn't *my* fault.
Too bad! They ought to have chosen a stronger tree.'
The two brown birds drooped their wings, and they said, 'Now we
shall only have two baby birds.'

Giraffe came stepping through the jungle trees. Now that the
storm had passed the sun was hot again, and Giraffe was looking
for some fresh green leaves to eat. When he came to the tree where
the brown birds lived, he saw the fresh green leaves that were
sheltering the nest. With his long, long neck he could easily reach
them. The two brown birds said, 'Please don't eat our leaves.
They are sheltering our two little eggs from the sun.'
But Giraffe went on eating the fresh green leaves until there was
only one leaf left, sheltering one of the brown birds' eggs.
And the sun shone hot on the other little egg till it cracked,
and dried into a burnt up shell.

Giraffe went away through the jungle and he said, 'It wasn't *my*
fault. Too bad! They ought to have built their nest higher up.'
The two brown birds were sad, and they said, 'Now we shall have
only one baby bird.'

Elephant came stamp, stamp, stamping through the jungle,
Elephant, the biggest of them all. The two brown birds said,
'Please don't stamp. Our tree isn't strong and safe any more.
It can't stand all that stamping. Please, please, Elephant.'
But Elephant came stamping to the tree, very close. And, because
he was tired, he leaned against the tree. He leaned against the tree
trunk with his great grey body.
The tree began to creak. It rustled all its leaves. It flung out its
branches and did its best to stand.
But the great grey heaviness of Elephant leaned harder.
Then cracking, creaking, thrashing, it fell.

The two brown birds flew away to a bush. They looked at their last little egg, which was broken. They looked at their nest, which was broken too. They said, 'Now we shall have no baby birds at all.' They were sad, so sad. Then Mother Brown Bird said, 'We *could* start again, with another four eggs.'
Father Brown Bird said, 'We'd have to choose another tree. We'd have to go searching for all those things we need, twigs and roots and moss and mud to build another nest. It would be too late, too late, too late.'

Elephant had listened to the brown birds talking. He said, 'It wasn't *my* fault. Too bad! They ought to have . . . ought to have . . . Well I don't know what they ought to have done . . .'
Elephant went to the edge of a pond, a wide stretch of water shining like a looking glass. He stood staring down, and he saw . . . himself, Elephant, the biggest of them all. And Elephant said in a very big voice, 'I'm big grey Elephant, the biggest of them all.'
Then Elephant said in a rather small voice:
'I'm big grey Elephant, the biggest of them all,
But the way I am behaving is very very small.
Am I small? No of course not. I'm big enough to say it,
I'm big enough to say that it *was* my fault.'
He went back, treading softly, to the fallen tree. The two brown birds were sitting in the bush. They were hiding their heads beneath their ruffled feathers.

Elephant said, 'Oh it *was* my fault. I'm big enough to say it. It *was* my fault.'
Then along came Monkey, and Rat, and Giraffe. And they said, 'Oh no! Not entirely *your* fault! It was all our faults, and we're very very sorry.'
Elephant thought for a moment, and he said, 'That's all very well, but being sorry's not enough. It *was* our fault, so now we'll put things right. The brown birds must start again, and this time we must help them. And the first thing we have to do is choose another tree.'
Monkey said, 'I'll choose one. I know about trees.'
Elephant said, 'Splendid, absolutely splendid! And now the birds need all those things to build another nest, twigs and roots and mud and moss.'
Monkey said, 'Well then! I'll collect the twigs.'
Rat said, 'Well then! I'll collect the roots.'

Giraffe said, 'Well then! I'll collect the moss.'
And Elephant said, 'Splendid! I'll collect the mud.'

While the birds chose a place in the tree for their nest, the animals
collected all the things that were needed, and put them down
in little heaps close to the tree trunk. Very soon the two brown
birds had built another nest. Then Mother Bird laid four new eggs,
four perfect little eggs.
Elephant said, 'Well, that's absolutely splendid. But last time,
because of us, the eggs got broken. So this time, because of us,
the eggs must not get broken. We'll guard the nest, day and night,
until the eggs hatch out.'
Monkey said, 'Well then! I'll guard it from above.'
Monkey sat down on a branch above the nest, to make sure
that nothing fell smash! to break the eggs.
Rat said, 'Well then! I'll guard it from below.'
Rat sat down at the bottom of the tree trunk, to show his sharp
white biting teeth if anyone came near.
Giraffe said, 'Well then! I'll guard it from behind.'
Giraffe stood behind the tree and stretched his long, long neck,
keeping a look-out for any sort of danger.
Elephant said, 'Splendid! I'll guard it from in front.'
Elephant stood in front of the tree, keeping it safe with his great
grey body. Now and again he said, 'Everybody listen.
I'm big grey Elephant, the biggest of them all,
But the way I was behaving was very very small.
We're putting things right now, so please keep away.
This tree's a special tree, it's guarded night and day.
Birds are hatching out here, so please don't touch.
Much obliged. Thank you. Thank you very much.'

Day and night, night and day, the animals kept watch, until at last
four tiny beaks came peck peck pecking. Then out of the egg shells
wriggled four baby birds.
Mother and Father Brown Bird were delighted. They said, 'Oh!
They're beautiful, absolutely beautiful. Thank you for helping us.
Our baby birds are beautiful.'
Elephant said, 'Well, that's absolutely splendid.'
And Monkey and Rat and Giraffe said, 'Splendid!'
After their long, careful guarding of the nest they were very, very
tired. And very, very happy!
Anita Hewett

Helpers

Who has helped you today?
Have you helped anyone?

Share and Share

Philip is walking to school past some new houses. He lives in a place called Greenham. Three years ago it was all fields. Now there are new roads, new red-brick houses, and even the trees are spindly new ones planted by the roadsides. There aren't many shops yet, but there is a big new school, and that's where Philip is going. He's thinking to himself as he walks along: 'It's a bit lonely here. We're the first children in the school, there's nobody older than us yet, so there are lots of empty classrooms. It's big and echoey. I used to go to a little school. There were cows in the field next to it, and a stream. We used to go for walks. And I knew everyone. But here it's so big, and empty. The school. The streets. The gardens. I don't really know anyone. My Mum doesn't know anyone. I wish my Dad hadn't had to change his job and come here.'

At the school gates Philip meets Mr. Chadwick, the headmaster.
'Hullo, Philip!'
'Hullo, Mr. Chadwick.'

Mr. Chadwick goes into his room and takes off his coat. He came from another town to be the headmaster of this new school.
Mr Chadwick is thinking to himself:
'I wish I hadn't come here. In my old school the classrooms were draughty and the playground was small and there was traffic roaring past all the time. But I knew everybody. I knew all the children's mums and dads, and the teachers and the cooks and the crossing ladies and all the people in the shops and houses round the school, and they knew me. Here, I've got a lovely new school with a big grass field for the children to play on. But I've been here in Greenham for nearly a year and I hardly know anybody. People don't seem to want to talk to each other in Greenham. Oh dear, I do hope everyone will be more friendly on Saturday when we go to Brightsand Bay.'

On Saturday, there's going to be a school outing. The children and their mums and dads, Mr. Chadwick and the teachers are all going on a trip to Brightsand Bay. Mr. Chadwick hopes it will help everyone to get to know each other better. Brightsand Bay is by the sea, it's a quiet little place, with lovely golden sands.

'I do hope it will be a sunny day,' thinks Mr. Chadwick. 'Then we can all get together and enjoy ourselves, we can have games on the beach, a sandcastle competition, and a great big picnic.'

Mr. Chadwick has ordered two coaches, and the mums and dads and teachers are going to get all the food ready the night before and pack it in big boxes – cakes, fruit, pies, bottles of coke and flasks of tea and coffee. Then no-one will have to carry heavy stuff around with them. The boxes will be put on the coaches, and as soon as they arrive at Brightsand Bay the food will be unpacked and they'll take it down to the beach for an enormous picnic.

On Saturday morning Philip gets up very early, but his mother is already downstairs getting his breakfast ready in the kitchen. She can't come on the outing because she has to look after Philip's baby sister. His father is working this weekend. So Philip is going alone.

Just as he is ready to leave his mother gives him two apples and a banana, a bar of chocolate and some sweets.
'Put these in your pockets, Philip, in case you get peckish.'
'But Mum!' says Philip, 'We don't have to take any food. It's all being taken on the coaches, ready for a picnic when we get there.'
'If I know you,' says his mother, 'you'll be as hungry as a hunter playing by the sea all day. These are just for you. Put them in your pockets. Now off you go. Mind how you cross the road. And have a good time!'

Outside the school, there's a noisy crowd of grown-ups and children. Two red motor coaches have their engines running. There's a pile of food boxes stacked up against the wall. Mr. Chadwick is ticking off people's names on his list. He is very busy and it's nearly time to go.

Some people don't hear him call their names. The Thomas family have all lost one another. The Simmonds children are still in the toilets. Philip gets into a coach before his name is called. 'Has anyone seen Philip Johnson?' shouts Mr. Chadwick. 'He'll be left behind if he doesn't come soon.'
'Here I am, on the coach!' calls Philip. But at last everything is sorted out and everyone is safely on board. Mr. Chadwick calls to the driver of the first coach: 'Right then, off we go!'

And there they go, on their way, off to the sea, to the sand, to the sun. Philip looks out of the window and wishes his Mum could have come, and hopes he'll find someone to play with on the beach.

And then, everything starts to go wrong. First the sun disappears behind a black cloud. It starts to rain. It pours down in torrents. So when they arrive at Brightsand Bay it certainly isn't bright, and the golden sands look like mud. Everyone sits inside the coaches, looking gloomily out of the streaming wet windows.

'Well,' says Mr. Chadwick, trying to cheer them up, 'Don't get too downhearted. We'll have our picnic now, inside the coaches. I expect all the children are starving. By the time we've had something to eat, perhaps the rain will have stopped.'

Everyone looks a little more cheerful, but when some of the dads go to get the boxes of food from the back of the coaches they can't find them. All the food has been left behind! In the bustle of getting on to the coaches, the boxes were left stacked up by the playground wall. There's nothing to eat or drink, and everyone is hungry. People begin to argue and to blame each other, especially they blame Mr. Chadwick. 'It's his fault,' they say, 'he forgot the food.' 'I'm sorry everyone,' says Mr. Chadwick.

What a miserable day it is! Pouring with rain, everyone hungry and nothing to eat. Instead of making people feel more friendly the trip to Brightsand Bay is making them cross.

Philip is just as fed up as everyone else. He sinks down into the big coach seat, and shoves his hands deep into his pockets, and mutters to himself: 'Rotten, miserable old Brightsands! Rotten, miserable old Greenham! I wish I'd never come to live in such a rotten place.'
His fingers curl round one of the apples in his pocket, and in the other one he feels the hard bar of chocolate.
'Oh well!' thinks Philip to himself. 'At least I've got the things to eat Mum gave me. I'm starving. I'll have a bit of chocolate. Better not let anyone see though.'
Philip thinks it wouldn't be fair to let the others see him eating when they haven't got anything. He begins to unwrap the chocolate carefully, inside his pocket.

Across the gangway from Philip a little girl called Jacqui is crying. Philip thinks, 'I wonder if she'd like a bit of my chocolate?' He leans

38

across the gangway to ask her, and Jacqui stops crying as soon as she sees the chocolate. Philip offers her mother some too. Then he pulls out his packet of sweets. 'Hey, Mr. Thomas, would you and Peter like some of my sweets?'
Mr. Thomas grins. 'Yes, thanks, Philip. But you must have some of our biscuits.'
Mrs. Simmonds starts rummaging in her carrier bag. 'I've got a packet of biscuits here somewhere. Would anyone like a biscuit?'

Soon lots of people are opening their bags or pulling things out of their pockets. Most people have brought something extra with them in case they should get hungry. They find sweets, fruit, packets of cheese, nuts, crisps, even packs of sandwiches and one person even has a large meat pie inside a sun hat! It turns out to be a very funny picnic! Soon everyone is sharing, everyone is talking and laughing; it's a real party!

By the time they've all had something to eat, the rain stops and the sun comes out. The sands are wet and shining, the sea sparkles, and everyone goes down to the beach. They paddle and swim, they play enormous games of rounders and football with forty-five on each side. They make gigantic sandcastles. Philip and Peter and Jacqui make one together and theirs is the biggest of all. While they are playing, the coach drivers go and buy supplies of tea and coke and coffee for everyone because they are all thirsty.

At last the happy day is over and the coaches are going home again. The mums and dads and teachers are all talking to each other, and keep changing places to speak to new friends. The children are playing *I Spy* and reading comics together and some of them are singing. Mr. Chadwick is walking along the gangway of the coach having a word with everyone and he stops beside Philip. 'Hullo, Philip, enjoy yourself today?'
'Yes, thanks,' says Philip sleepily. 'It was great.'
'I hope you had some of your own sweets,'
says Mr. Chadwick, laughing.
'Mm. Yes, thank you, I had such a lot of things from everyone else too.'
Mr Chadwick grins at him. 'It's been a good day – Greenham's not such a bad place, is it Philip?'
'No, not bad,' says Philip. 'Not bad at all.'

Geoffrey Curtis

The Robinsons Go on Holiday

The Robinsons were waiting for the holidays to come. Dad and Mum, and the two children – Nicholas and Deborah – were waiting and waiting, looking forward to going on holiday. Two whole weeks at Sandy Bay!

When Dad came home from the factory, he said, 'Only three more days to Saturday. Then we'll be on holiday. No more work!'
Next day, when Mum had finished the washing, she said, 'Only two more days to Saturday. Then we'll be on holiday. No more work!'
The day after that, when the children came home, they said, 'Only one more day to Saturday. School's broken up and we're going on holiday. No more work! No more work!'
The Robinson's tabby cat cleaned her whiskers. All *she* said was: '*Miaow, miaow!*' She wasn't going on holiday. The lady next door would be looking after her. Pussy Matilda couldn't stop working because she never *did* any work. She spent her time being a Pussy Matilda.

At last it was Saturday. Dad got the car out. Into the boot went two big cases, the picnic basket, buckets and spades, and all the other bits and pieces.
'Right! That's that,' said Dad. 'Come along. What's your Mum doing? Come on, Mum.'
Mum sighed as she got in the car: 'Oh dear! I'm sure I must have forgotten something. Did I turn off the gas? I must have done. But I didn't have time to clean the oven.'
Dad started the engine: 'It's too late now. Much too late to think about housework.
The Robinsons are on their way.
No more work for *us* today.'

After some time they came to the motorway. Dad drove fast on the smooth, wide road. Until they got stuck behind a lorry!
'Pass it, pass it, Dad,' said Nicholas.

'No, Dad. No, you can't,' said Mum.

Deborah said, 'Aren't lorries a nuisance! Can't the driver go faster?'

Dad shook his head: 'He's only doing his job. Just because *we're* on holiday, it doesn't mean other people don't have to work. We can't all be Pussy Matildas you know. Which reminds me, when we get to a garage, I hope the garage man is working. If I don't get petrol the car won't go. So we'll have to walk a hundred miles, and we shan't get to Sandy Bay till Christmas.'

Mum said, 'I should *never* get there, not with these high-heeled sandals I'm wearing.'

When they came to the end of the motorway, to an ordinary road, they stopped at a garage. A notice said: OPEN.

And Dad said 'Good! No Pussy Matildas here, thank goodness!'

Dad put four gallons of petrol in the tank, then went to the office in the garage to pay. When he came back he said, 'There you are! The man in the garage was working today, To help the Robinsons on their way.'

Before very long they came to the country. They drove along between green fields where brown and white cows were grazing. Mum looked at her watch: 'It's time for elevenses. Can't we stop for a cup of tea?' Dad said, 'I can only see cows, not cafés.'

'But last year,' said Mum. 'When we came this way, we stopped for some tea at the top of a hill, up on that big open space, the moor, where the heather grows. Are we anywhere near it?'

'Near enough!' said Dad. 'Here's the hill.'

Nicholas thought for a moment, then he said, 'I remember, Mum. The tea van was there. A van turned into a sort of shop. And a lady selling cups of tea, and coke, and crisps, and chocolate and stuff.'

'That's right,' said Mum.

'There it is!' shouted Deborah. 'Look, Dad. By the side of the road.'

'I do hope it's open.' Mum sounded worried. 'If it isn't I'll die. I'm terribly thirsty. I remembered the food for our picnic lunch. And I filled the thermos with tea and forgot it! Unless I have a cup of tea, I can't go another, single mile.'

Dad pulled in to the side of the road. 'Do you hear that, children? If the tea van's not open, if the tea lady isn't working today, we'll have to leave your Mum behind, all among the heather and the birds and the rabbits.'

Nicholas laughed. 'Poor old Mum!'
And Deborah shouted, 'It's open. It's open!'

The tea lady smiled, and Dad said, 'Good morning. Lovely morning!
Two teas, please. And a couple of cokes for the children. Thank you.'
Mum said, 'This will save my life.'
The tea lady nodded: 'It's freshly made. Nothing like a cup of tea to
help you on your way.'
As they started off again in the car, Dad said, 'There you are you see.
The tea van lady was working today,
To help the Robinsons on their way.'

After they had driven across the moor, and stopped to have their
picnic lunch, and gone down a hill to a little village, Dad pulled in
to the side of the road and stopped the car.
'Better have a look at the map, I think. There are two ways now to
Sandy Bay, a big main road and a narrower one that winds about.
I wonder which is better.'
'Wouldn't the main road be quicker?' said Mum.
'It depends on the traffic, all those lorries,' said Dad. 'Look! That's
lucky. A policeman's coming, on a bicycle. He'll be sure to know.'
Mum said, 'Perhaps he isn't on duty. Not working. Just going
home for his dinner!'
Nicholas looked at the tall policeman. 'He doesn't look *much* like a
Pussy Matilda.'
'Nicholas, be quiet!' said Dad. Then he called, 'Excuse me, Officer.'
The policeman stopped, and crossed the road.
'Afternoon, Sir. What's the trouble?'
'Afternoon,' said Dad. 'Can you help us? Which is the best way
to Sandy Bay? The big main road and the by-pass I suppose.'
The policeman shook his head. 'Not today, Sir. There's a lorry
overturned at the roundabout. Nobody hurt, but it's blocking
the road. Traffic's held up for miles, I'm afraid. Better go the other
way. The road's a bit rough, but you'd still get there quicker.'
As Dad started off again, he said, 'Well, there you are, you see.
The village policeman was working today,
To help the Robinsons on their way.'

But when they were driving on the narrow, rough road, Dad said,
'Goodness! This road is bumpy. We shan't get to Sandy Bay for
hours. All these wretched holes! The road needs repairing. It's time
some work was done on this road.'

And then, around the very next corner, they saw a sign saying:
ROAD WORKS AHEAD. The road repair men stopped their work for a
minute to look at the car, and the children waved. The men waved
back, and smiled. Except one!
Deborah said, 'He's grumpy, that one.'
And Mum said, 'I'd be grumpy too, if I had to work on a day
like this.'

Ahead of them now the road was smoother, and when they came
to the top of a hill, Nicholas shouted, 'Look! There's the sea.'
They drove nearer and nearer to Sandy Bay.
'Downhill now, all the way,' smiled Dad.
'Thank goodness we're nearly there,' said Mum.

And because other people had worked that day,
To help the Robinsons on their way,
They came at last to Sandy Bay.
And had a lovely holiday!

Anita Hewett

Playing in Wind and Rain

Do you like playing with water and sand and mud?
Do you like the sound of the wind?

Mud Pies

In my garden there's a place
I make mud pies
Lovely slippy, sloppy pies!
Water from the watering can,
And Spot, our dog, she digs the earth,
And splish, splash, splosh the water on
And pit pat, pit pat
Shape the pie.
Not pies to eat though
Or I might die.
Pies for splatting,
Pies for patting,
Pies for smoothing,
Pies for squeezing,
Oozing, slippy, sloppy,
Plopping
Lovely mud pies!

Elizabeth Lindsay

Windy Day

It's a windy day
Just right for washing,
We'll peg the washing on the line.
There's Grandad's trousers
Susan's socks
Grandma's bloomers and some shirts
And a jolly great big sheet.
Put the pegs on
One two three.

Dad's pyjamas – they're off.
After them, after them!
They've got away
They're up in the air
Turning over and over
Is someone inside them?
The wind is. The wind is!
Come back pyjamas.
I'll get them.

They're stuck in that tree
There's a stick in the leg
No, they're off over there
They're behind the hedge
I'll get them –
And now they're all dirty
I'll have to wash them again.

Elizabeth Lindsay

The Wind and My Kite

Last night I heard the wind call
And rattle the door, leading into the hall,
Lost in the dark all forlorn and alone
It breezed round the house in a soft low moan.
So I'm flying my kite
So the wind's got a friend
And they dance and they dance
And dance without end.

Elizabeth Lindsay

45

It's a Rainy Day

Shiny pavement on the ground,
Each lorry makes a swishing sound,
Water plants splash in the street,
And puddles part beneath my feet;
It's a rainy day.

Old boots now look wet and new,
My coat is changing colour too,
And in the park the dust has gone,
The plants have got their jewels on;
It's a rainy day.

Catching raindrops on my tongue
Is tasting where the clouds come from,
I clean my knees by running fast
In all the longest wet mop grass
On a rainy day.

When it stops the fun is gone
Although the wetness lingers on,
But puddles give a sudden peep
Into a world beneath my feet
On a rainy day.

Rainy day,
Sounds of summer in the rain.
Come and play,
It's a rainy day.

Sarah McNeill

Out in the Rain

I like being out in the rain
I've got my boots on
And my mac
And shiny yellow sou'wester hat.
My rain coat
Keeps me nice and dry
Until I look up at the sky.

We jump in puddles
Hand in hand
And churn the mud up
As we land.
We run in circles
Round and round
And slip upon
The shiny ground.
And when it stops,
The falling rain,
It brings to an end
Our laughing game.

Elizabeth Lindsay

Let Me In

'Let me in',
Called the wind
Down the chimney at dusk.
'Let me in, let me in,
Let me in and I'll just
Whisper softly and dance you
A jig on the floor,
And if you will join in
We will dance more and more . . .
If you'd please let me in' said the wind.

'Let me in',
Whined the wind
At the window all night,
'Let me in, let me in,
Let me in and I might
Let you win at a game
We can play on the stairs,
Whooping loudly and howling
And shouting, 'Who cares!'
If you'd please let me in', said the wind.

'Let me in'
Cried the wind
Through the keyhole at dawn,
'Let me in, let me in,
Let me in, for I've sworn
To be quiet in the house
And to let the dust lie
And just sleep in a corner
Till mischief comes by . . .

Then we'll leap
Up together
And roar down the stairs,
Whirling out to the yard and
Then back past the chairs
Making waves in the curtains
And carpets for fun,
Letting fly with the papers
To make the cat run . . .

If you'd please let me in,
Won't you please let me in?
I'm so lonely,
If you'd only let me in', said the wind.

Sarah McNeill

The Giant of the Sky

Listen to me blow
I am the giant of the sky
Hear me puff and puff and blow.

I shoo the clouds across the sky
Pick up the leaves and make them fly
Listen to me blow.

Sometimes from ice lands I come
Blowing in snow clouds dark and grey
And then I shake and shake them hard
So snowflakes whirl and fall away
To cover the land in freezing white.

And sometimes on soft summer days
When the sun bakes the earth in rippling haze
I murmur softly among the leaves
And blow a coolness with my breeze.

Listen, listen to me blow
I am a secret to come and go
Unseen and terrible when I moan
I howl in the sky huge and alone
And sometimes I whisper as I pass by
A gentle giant in the sky.

I am a secret to come and go
Where do I come from
Where do I go?
That is a secret that nobody knows.

Elizabeth Lindsay

Round and Round

Does everything have a pattern . . . a beginning, a growing and a start-again?

The Dandelion

A dandelion grew beside the path leading to the shops. Instead of a yellow flower it had a soft white puff-ball of seeds. A boy saw it when he was out with his mother. 'Look,' he said, 'a dandelion clock.' He knew that if you blew once and all the seeds flew away, then it was one o'clock (dandelion time, that is) but if you had to blow three or even four times then it was three o'clock or four o'clock. His mother said 'What's the time, Kevin? Blow it and see'. Kevin blew once. 'One o'clock' he said. He blew twice. 'Two o'clock.' By this time most of the soft feather seeds had drifted away but there were still a few left so he blew again, hard.
'Three o'clock. Is it really three o'clock?'
'Half-past two,' said his mother. 'Not bad for a dandelion clock. I wonder where all those seeds will land? I wish the wind could just pick us up like the seeds and drop us outside the supermarket. Come on.'

The dandelion seeds on their tiny feathery parachutes were carried by the wind into all sorts of places. One landed on a baby's hat and was wheeled into the supermarket in a pushchair. One floated into a shopping bag and was taken for a ride on a bus. Others floated over a school playground and some of the children tried to catch them – they called the floating seeds 'fairies'. If you caught one it was supposed to bring you luck, but the seeds weren't easy to catch as they danced on the wind.

One of the seeds floated over hedges and walls and down into a garden. The tiny seed dropped to the ground and lay resting against a leaf. When a ginger cat came along and scratched up a shower of earth, some of it fell on the dandelion seed, covering it completely. Now it lay safe and warm in a bed of brown earth with a coverlet of dry leaves.

As the days passed, down there, underground in the darkness where worms glided past, the seed began to put down roots and to push a shoot up to the surface. The tiny seed acted as a kind of Control Centre, sending information to the roots telling them which way was down, and to the shoot telling it which way was up.

51

If it could have spoken it might have said, 'This is Dandelion control, Dandelion control. Greenshoot launch in 10 seconds dandelion time. Countdown begins – ten, nine, eight, seven, six, five, four, three, two, one, zero. Lift Off! We have lift off! Greenshoot is on its way!'

Up and up went the shoot, slowly by our time, but dandelion time is different from ours. When the April rain came there was already a tuft of leaves above the ground.

Fat drops of rain splashed down on the path and dripped from the bushes. The ginger cat who was out in the garden began to get very wet and he ran to his front door and miaowed loudly, his wet ears drooping. The children who lived in the house opened the door and let him in.
'Oh, look! Poor pussycat,' said the girl.
'Mum, he's soaked,' called the boy.
'Keep him there till I get a towel,' shouted their mother from the kitchen, 'or he'll make everything wet and muddy.'
When she came, carrying a towel, they rubbed the ginger cat softly and dried his paws. 'As it's so wet,' she said, 'you'd better wear your wellingtons to school – and you'll need an umbrella too.'
'Poor pussycat,' said the little girl, 'he needed an umbrella today.'
When it was time to go to school they splashed along the path, each holding a brightly coloured umbrella. They liked the rain: so did the dandelion. Its leaves made a kind of upside down umbrella to catch the raindrops and channel them down to the roots below.

When the bright sunny days of spring came the garden was full of yellow flowers – daffodils, crocuses, celandines – and the dandelion, too, put out a yellow flower, like a bright round face, lifted up to the sun.

In the evening when the sun set and a blackbird sang a bedtime song, the dandelion flower folded itself up for the night, just as the children folded up their clothes (sometimes) before they went to bed.

Soon spring changed to summer and the warm days of summer were a very busy time for everything in the garden. Everything was eating. Hundreds of small mouths were biting, chewing and munching at the green leaves. Slugs and snails chewed at the lettuces, caterpillars nibbled cabbages, everything seemed to be
52

eating. Fortunately for the dandelion none of the creatures in the garden liked the rather hot taste of dandelion leaves and luckily there were no rabbits or guinea pigs living near, because they like dandelion leaves very much. So the dandelion plant didn't get eaten, but there were other dangers.

The children in whose garden the dandelion lived often came out to play there now, and the ginger cat came with them. The children had a ping-pong ball which they bounced towards the cat and he caught it every time. 'He'd make a good goal-keeper,' said the boy. 'Nothing gets past him.'

Their father came over to them. 'You're going to have to move, all of you,' he said. 'I'm going to cut the grass.'
'Oh, you'll cut all the daisies,' said the girl.
'Don't worry, they'll soon grow again,' said her father.
'Let me pick some first,' she said, 'and I'll make a daisy-chain.'
'Let's make a daisy-chain for the cat,' said the boy. 'Get as many as you can.'

So they picked all the daisies they could find for the daisy-chain. They wondered if they should pick the dandelion flower as well but then they remembered that the dandelion stem was hollow with a sort of sticky juice inside.
'A dandelion won't be any good,' said the girl. 'Daisies are best.'

So the dandelion stayed unpicked and the cat looked very smart in a daisy-chain which he wore over one ear while he was sleeping.

When their father had finished cutting the lawn the grass cuttings were placed in a heap in the corner of the garden near where the dandelion grew. Leaves and garden rubbish were piled there, too. A wandering hedgehog looking for a home made himself a bed under the grass and leaves. The dandelion marked the place where he went in and out. But now the dandelion looked different. Instead of having a round yellow flower face it looked as if it had a head of soft white hair. As soon as the children saw the puff-ball of feathery seeds, they ran to pick the dandelion and blow the seeds away. They blew once, twice, three and four times before all the seeds had floated away. By dandelion time it was time for the new dandelion seeds to set off and find themselves a home, where they could grow.

Zoë Bailey

53

Dandelion

Dandelion in the grass
Sees the children play
Hides its face when thunder shouts
And children go away.

Dandelion in the grass
Golden as the sun
Time will change your yellow head
Your hair will whiten soon.

Dandelion in the grass
Hears the children say –
'Look, a dandelion clock,
We'll blow the time away.'

Zoë Bailey

Dandelion is from the French words *dents de lion*
which means lion's teeth. Think of the jagged
edges of the leaves, white with frost.

Everything Starts Again

Once upon upon a time there was a big green field. In the field lived
a brown and white cow.
In a corner of the field there was a shiny green pond. In the pond
lived a little black tadpole.
Beside the pond grew a poppy flower, with delicate, bright red
petals.
Over the pond flew a yellow brimstone butterfly.
Close to the pond, in an oak tree, lived a blackbird.
The oak tree was very, very old.

One morning in the springtime, when the brown and white cow
was standing by the pond, she heard a little voice. The bubbly little
voice was coming from the water. Cow looked down and saw the
wriggly tadpole.
Tadpole said, 'Oh! Mrs Cow, I do feel strange. I thought I was a
tadpole, but every now and then I feel as though I'm changing into
something else. It's really quite surprising, so please can you
explain why I'm changing from a tadpole to . . . I don't know what?'

Cow spoke kindly to the puzzled little tadpole: 'Moo! I've always
thought every tadpole knew. *Every* little tadpole changes
as it grows.'
Tadpole's tail wriggled. 'My tail is getting shorter. I'm growing
little legs at the back. Is this right?'
Mrs Cow said, 'Moo! You'll grow front legs too, and your tiny tail
will almost disappear. You'll change to a small green frog, when
it's time, and then you'll come out of the water, and you'll hop.'
Tadpole wriggled, and Mrs Cow went on: 'Moo! Yes it's true.
You'll grow bigger and bigger, until you are a fully grown, fine
mother frog.'
'Really?' said the tadpole. 'And what happens next?'
Mrs Cow said, 'Moo! You will make something new. You'll lay lots
and lots of eggs, like tiny black dots, all wrapped around in jelly
stuff to keep them safe from harm. And then, when the time comes,
the tiny black eggs will begin to grow larger.'

Tadpole bubbled with excitement: 'And make new little tadpoles?'
'Moo! Yes they do. Everything starts again, you see, in the same
proper pattern, all over again. A beginning, and a growing, and a
new start again. Tadpoles grow to frogs, and frogs lay eggs, and
eggs make new tadpoles, and the tadpoles grow to frogs, and the
frogs lay eggs, and the eggs make more new tadpoles, and . . .'

Cow would have gone on for ever and ever, but Tadpole stopped
her. 'Excuse me Mrs Cow. Does everyone have a proper pattern
like that? A beginning, and a growing, and a new start again? For
instance, does red poppy have a pattern?'
Cow said, 'Moo! Most of us do. Different sorts of patterns! Why
don't you ask her?'

Tadpole spoke politely to the proud red poppy: 'Excuse me, Poppy.
Do you have a pattern?'
Poppy tossed her head: 'I'm a flower, don't you know? All flowers
have a pattern. I've got petals, as you see. But my beautiful petals
will fall, when it's time. Then my seed box will grow. It's rather
like a pepper pot, with holes around the top. When the wind blows
my stalk to and fro, to and fro, out of those holes will come . . .'
'Pepper?' said the tadpole.
Poppy tossed her head: 'Silly little Tadpole! Out of my seed box
come tiny black poppy seeds. They lie in the earth and wait until

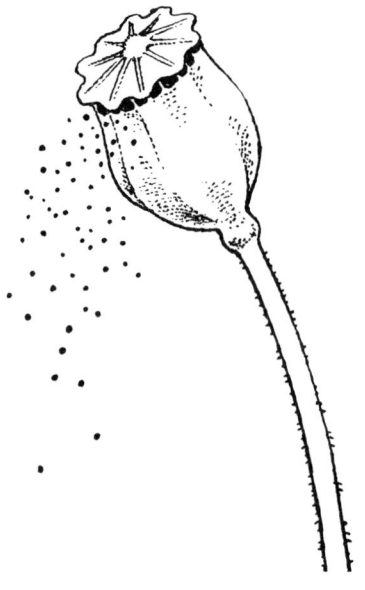

the time comes, the right time, the springtime, and then they start to grow. They grow into poppies again, like me.'

Tadpole understood: 'Then *their* petals fall off again, and the seed boxes grow again. The seeds come shaking out again, and the seeds begin to grow again. Everything starts again and *again*.'

Poppy's head nodded in the breeze. Then Tadpole listened. He heard a small voice above the water, and it said, 'I flutter by, I flutter by, because I am a butterfly.'

Tadpole said, 'Does Butterfly have a pattern too?'

Butterfly answered for herself, and she said, 'Of course I have a pattern. I started with an egg. Out of the egg I came crawling, crawling, a fine little caterpillar. That's how I started. Then, in the winter, I wrapped myself up in a little silken parcel, and I waited, very still. And then, when the time came, the right time, the springtime, out came the sunshine, and out came I. I unfolded myself from my silken parcel. I unfolded my wings, and I changed to a butterfly.'

Tadpole looked at the lovely yellow butterfly. 'You?' he said. 'A caterpillar? Crawling?'

Butterfly fluttered her yellow wings. 'If you wait and you watch you will see,' she said. 'I shall lay some eggs of my own when the time comes. And out of those eggs will come crawling, crawling . . .'

Tadpole interrupted: 'New little caterpillars?'

'Right, little Tadpole.' Butterfly was pleased. 'And they'll wrap themselves up in their little silken parcels, and then unfold themselves as butterflies, like me, to flutter by, flutter by, every little butterfly. And now I shall flutter to that branch up there. If you'll excuse me, I want to talk to Blackbird.'

Tadpole called, 'Tell me, does Blackbird have a pattern?'

'A pattern?' said Blackbird. 'Of course I have a pattern.
All blackbirds have a pattern.

Baby blackbirds come from eggs,
And baby blackbirds grow.
When they've grown they lay more eggs.
As everyone should know.
From those eggs new blackbirds come,
And then *those* blackbirds grow.
When they've grown *they* lay more eggs.
It always will be so.'

Tadpole was excited: 'It's so wonderful. So clever! It starts again and starts again, round and round and round.'

The oak tree rustled: 'Sh! little Tadpole. Don't get so excited. If you'd lived as long as I have you'd have seen it all before. Day after day I've seen the proper patterns, year after year, through the springtime and the summer and the autumn and the winter.'

'But when does it *begin*, Mr Oak Tree?' asked the Tadpole.

'When?' said the oak tree. 'People say in springtime. That's when my leaf buds begin to wake up. Butterflies unfold their wings. Seeds begin to grow. Baby blackbirds come from eggs. And little tadpoles wriggle.'

'And after the springtime?' said Tadpole. 'What comes next?'

'Summer,' said the oak tree. 'When everything is growing. That's when my buds have unfolded into leaves. Everything is flowering and fluttering and flying. And swimming and hopping – that's if you're a frog!'

'And after the summer?' said Tadpole. 'What comes after?'

'Autum,' said the oak tree. 'The getting ripe and ready time. That's when my acorns fall to the ground. Seeds fall down to the earth in the autumn, so that things can start growing all over again. But of course you have to wait, through the cold dark winter. My branches are bare in the winter,' said the oak tree. 'People say, dead! Things are dead in the winter! But things are only sleeping, waiting for the springtime.'

'Then everything starts again,' said the tadpole.

The very old oak tree rustled its leaves: 'Who am I to say when it all starts again. *I* think it just goes around and around. Like the world itself, around and around! And now the sun is setting, so it's time for us to sleep.'

'Goodnight,' said the tadpole. 'I shall see you in the morning.' Then Tadpole wriggled to her place in the water weeds, to sleep through the darkness and wait for the morning, and the sun that would start another day.

Anita Hewett

Taking Care

We share the world with everything that's alive.
Can you care for the place where you live and those
who share it with you?

The Slubberdegullion

Once upon a time there was a Slubberdegullion.
The Slubberdegullion was small and round and fat. He had two
little arms and two little legs, and a chubby pink face.
And he lived in a nest!

The Slubberdegullion's nest was on the ground, among tall green
trees in a wood. It was soft and round and comfy, made of twigs and
moss and feathers, and the Slubberdegullion's fat little body fitted
in neatly when he went to bed at night.

One sunny day in summer, when he woke up in the morning, the
Slubberdegullion got ready for a picnic. Into his basket he put a big
tin of fizzy lemonade and some sandwiches, carefully wrapped in
paper bags. Five of them were cheese and pickle, five of them were
treacle.
Then he put on his little black boots. He always wore them. And he
put on his green woolly hat. He always wore that. Then the
Slubberdegullion went through the village, past the Cosy Café,
and over the playing field, where people were taking their dogs for
a walk. He went along a road and stopped for a minute to look at
Mrs Haggetty's tidy little house, and her tidy little garden full of
marigolds and pinks. He walked across the park, between the beds
of roses. Then he climbed to the top of a grassy little hill, and sat
down and started on his sandwiches.
He ate all five of the cheese and pickle sandwiches, and put the
greasy paper bags back in the basket. 'Those were good and tasty!'
he said. 'Now I'll try the treacle ones.'
He ate four treacle sandwiches, patted his tummy, and said,
'Oh dear! I'll never eat the last one.'
He put the last one back in the basket, and took out the tin of
lemonade. After he had drunk the fizzy lemonade, he put the
empty tin back into the basket, and lay on his back with his hands
on his tummy. Then he fell fast asleep until the sun went down.
When a fresh wind blew, the Slubberdegullion woke from his sleep
and said, 'Time to go home!'

Away he went, down the hill with his basket, home towards his comfortable nest.

As the Slubberdegullion walked across the park, along the little path between the rose beds, he looked in his basket and he said, 'Those greasy paper bags! They're only rubbish. *I* don't want them.' And he threw the paper bags down among some yellow roses. Then on he went, home towards his nest.

After the Slubberdegullion had gone, the park keeper saw the paper bags, and he said, 'Well! *I* don't want them. I'd better pick them up before they blow along the path. It must be that Slubberdegullion again.
He doesn't seem to understand that tidiness is best,
so I'll pick up all his rubbish and I'll take it to his nest.'

Meanwhile, the Slubberdegullion was passing Mrs Haggetty's tidy little house, and her tidy little garden full of marigolds and pinks. He looked in his basket and he said, 'That treacle sandwich! It's only rubbish. *I* don't want it.'
And he threw the treacle sandwich in the middle of the marigolds. Then on he went, home towards his nest.

After the Slubberdegullion had gone, Mrs Haggetty saw the treacle sandwich, and she said, 'Well! *I* don't want it. I'd better pick it up before the wasps come and settle on it. It must be that Slubberdegullion again.
He doesn't seem to understand that tidiness is best,
so I'll pick up all his rubbish and I'll take it to his nest.'

Meanwhile, the Slubberdegullion was walking across the playing field. He looked in his basket, and he said, 'That empty tin! It's only rubbish. *I* don't want it.' And he threw the lemonade tin down on the grass. Then on he went, home towards his nest.

After the Slubberdegullion had gone, over the field came a boy and a girl, taking their little dog Rover for a walk. They saw the empty tin, and they said, 'Well! *We* don't want it. We'd better pick it up before it cuts poor Rover's paw. It must be that Slubberdegullion again.
He doesn't seem to understand that tidiness is best,
so we'll pick up all his rubbish and we'll take it to his nest.'

Meanwhile, the Slubberdegullion was walking in the village towards the Cosy Café. His basket was empty now. And so was his tummy. So he went inside the cafe and had sausages and chips and a big mug of tea for his supper. He said, 'That was delicious, perfectly delicious. Now it's home for me, to my comfortable nest.'

But when he got home to his nest . . . oh dear! When he got home to his nest . . . oh my!
In his nest were the greasy paper bags, the sticky treacle sandwich, the empty tin of fizzy lemonade.
Around his nest stood the park keeper, Mrs Haggetty, the boy and the girl. And Rover!
Beside the nest stood a great big shiny thing, rather like the shape of the lemonade tin, but much, much bigger, with a lid on top.

The Slubberdegullion was not at all pleased.
'How can I sleep in my nest, I'd like to know. Its full of horrid
rubbish. Yuck-yuck-yucketty!'
Then they all said, 'Oh! But it's yours, you see.
You didn't seem to understand that tidiness is best,
so we picked up all your rubbish and we brought it to your nest.'
The Slubberdegullion said, 'So I see. And whatever is that great
big tin you've brought me? I want to go to sleep in my comfortable
nest. I don't want to sleep in a great big tin.'
Then they all said, 'That's not for sleeping. It's for rubbish.
When you go on picnics, *we* don't want your rubbish. So we've
brought you a rubbish bin. A bin to put your rubbish in!'

The Slubberdegullion understood at last. He went to his nest and
began to clear it out. The greasy paper bags blew away among the
trees. He had to run to catch them. Then he put them in the bin.

Next, he picked up the sticky treacle sandwich. A wasp that had
settled on it buzzed around his nose. But he put the treacle
sandwich in the bin.

The empty lemonade tin nearly cut his finger. But he managed
to put it in the bin.

Then his nest was clean and tidy, and they all said, 'There! That's
the way to do it. So when you go on picnics:
If you see a bin,
put the rubbish in.
If there's not a bin about
take the rubbish home.'

Then they smiled at him, and said, 'Goodnight. Sleep well.'
The Slubberdegullion settled in his comfy nest. 'That's the way
to do it. Now I understand.'
Then he yawned three times, and went to sleep.

The Slubberdegullion still goes on picnics. But he never throws
his rubbish down where people don't want it.
If he sees a bin,
he puts the rubbish in.
If there's not a bin about
he takes the rubbish home.

Anita Hewett

Slugs Crossing

On their way to school each morning Sally and her mother walked along a footpath beside a building site. New houses were being built on what had once been wild waste ground covered with blackberry bushes. Now all that was left of the wildness was a few straggly bushes and weeds beside the path. But when it had been raining there was a wet green smell that Sally liked. The only thing was, the rain seemed to bring out the slugs and they liked to ooze across the path just where people walked. Sally's mother didn't like slugs one little bit.

'Oh,' she said unhappily, stepping over one. 'I don't like slugs.'
'There's a little white one over here,' said Sally.
'Don't tell me,' said her mother, 'I don't want to see.'
'Mind there's one there!'
Sally's mother hopped on one foot trying not to tread on a slug. 'Where?'
'Oh no,' said Sally. 'It's only a stick. Why don't you like slugs?'
'I don't know really,' said her mother. 'I suppose I don't like their softness and squelchiness.'
'There's a big one,' shouted Sally, 'look.'
'No I can't,' said her mother closing her eyes.
'It's got an orange stripe down it's side,' went on Sally, looking at the slug curiously. 'I think it's dead though.'
Safely past the slug her mother opened her eyes. 'Poor thing – all those feet tramping along the path – must be difficult for the slugs to get across.'
'I know,' said Sally. 'I'll be a slug detector for you. I'll go *'beep beep beep'* slowly when there aren't any slugs and *'beep-beep-beep'* very quickly when I see one.'
So they walked on, Sally beeping loudly whenever she saw a slug.

When they left the footpath Sally and her mother had a busy road to cross before they could get to the school, but there was a lollipop lady to stop the traffic so that children could cross safely. She held up a lollipop-shaped sign that said 'Children Crossing' and all the cars stopped. Then she beckoned the children and their mothers across the road.

'Come on, Sally,' said her mother. 'We can cross now.'

Sally looked thoughtful. 'That's what the slugs need.'

'What?' said her mother.

'A lollipop lady,' said Sally, 'so they can get across the path safely.'

'That's true,' said her mother. 'Look you'd better run on now, or you'll be late.'

'Kiss first,' said Sally. 'Mind the slugs when you go back.'

'I think I'll go back another way,' said her mother.

Later that morning, in school, Sally drew a picture. It showed a family of slugs crossing a path and her mother with one foot in the air trying not to tread on them. Sally asked her teacher for the words 'Careful – Slugs Crossing' and wrote them underneath.

At lunchtime Sally went to look at Class 3's white rabbit. It had an enclosure on the grass all to itself and it came up to be stroked when you called it. Class 3 didn't like anyone else touching it though.

A boy from Class 3 came up to Sally and said, 'Don't give it any grass.'

'I'm not. I just wanted to stroke it,' said Sally, feeling the softness of the rabbit's white fur under her fingers.

'It doesn't want to be stroked,' said the boy sulkily.

'How do *you* know?' answered Sally.

Just then Sally's teacher, Miss Newbury, came up to them, looking flustered. 'Children,' she said, 'let me know if you see our gerbil anywhere. She's got out of her cage again. If you see a tail or a whisker where a tail or a whisker shouldn't be –'

Sally interrupted, 'She got in the waste paper basket last time she escaped.'

'Well, she's not there now,' said Miss Newbury, 'and she's not in the Wendy house, not in among the paint pots and not here with the rabbit, so I can't think where she can be. Anyway, if you see her, come and tell me. Don't rush up to her. She'll only run away again. All right?'

'Yes, Miss,' said the two children.

When Miss Newbury had gone the boy from Class 3 said, 'Perhaps the gerbil's hiding in Miss Newbury's desk and she'll jump out when Miss calls the register.' They both giggled at the thought of that.

But when the register was called no gerbil popped out: the only excitement was Nikos rushing in noisily.

'Please, Miss', he said, 'there's a mouse in the boys' toilet!'

Miss Newbury looked up at once, 'A what?'

Nikos hesitated, 'Well it looked like a mouse.'

'Ah,' said Miss Newbury, 'show me.' Almost at once she was back, and there between her hands was the missing gerbil. 'It wasn't a mouse, it was the gerbil, naughty thing,' she said. The gerbil looked out at the children with bright black eyes from the cage of her hands. They crowded round to stroke the tiny head.

'Put her back in the cage now, Nikos,' said Miss Newbury. Nikos carefully put the little gerbil inside its cage – while the other gerbil, who never escaped, began pulling the straw in the cage into an untidy heap and then disappeared inside it. The children gathered round to watch. Sally watched too – the gerbils were so soft and quick. But she thought to herself, 'I bet we wouldn't be watching them if they were slugs. Nobody cares about slugs. Nobody.'

That evening after tea, Sally had an idea. She got out her crayons and a sheet of paper and set to work. When she'd finished she asked her mother for some sellotape and went outside. When she came indoors again she wiped her wellingtons on the mat with a happy smile.

The next morning when Sally and her mother reached the footpath, there, sellotaped to a tree, was a notice in large red crayon letters.

It said 'Careful – Slugs Crossing'.

'I did that so people would be careful and not tread on them' said Sally. 'Poor slugs.'

'Quite right,' said her mother, 'that was a very good idea, but I think I'd rather go another way.'

'It's quicker this way,' said Sally. 'Don't worry, I'll be your slug detector – *beep beep beep* – there's one – *beep-beep-beep*.'

And detecting every single slug she led her mother carefully along the path.

Zoë Bailey

Brave and Gentle Shepherds

What does a shepherd do? When does he work?
Why does he need clever dogs to help him?
Would you like to take care of a baby lamb?

Grandfather and His Dog

Clive was a little boy who went to school in the village. When school was over he would walk home with his friends, but one by one his friends would go into their houses and Clive would climb the long hill up to his own house. It was a farm, and Clive lived there with his Grand-dad. Clive would reach the end of the lane, then he'd swing open the gate into the big field, and then he'd run all the way into the yard.

Sometimes his Grand-dad would be working near the farm-house. But sometimes he would be up on the green mountain, with his clever sheep-dogs. For Clive's Grand-dad was a shepherd, a man who kept lots of sheep. Clive would stand at the bottom of the mountain and look high up. He could see his Grand-dad there, so far away that he looked the size of a doll, and the white sheep no bigger than little white balls of wool. Clive could hear his Grand-dad whistling to his dogs, as he sent them racing over the mountain to gather the sheep together. Oh, they were clever dogs! A shepherd has to have clever dogs.

'Come by, Sam!' Clive would hear his Grand-dad shout, 'Stay, Bess!' His voice would sound far away, but Sam and Bess, the two black and white sheep-dogs could hear everything, they would obey the shouts and whistles, and safely guide the sheep wherever Clive's Grand-dad wanted them.

It was lovely on the mountain, with the dogs and the bleating sheep, up there in the wind. Clive would have liked to go there every day and help his Grand-dad, but he could only go on Saturdays and Sundays, or in the school holidays.

One day Clive came home from school. He opened the gate into the big field, raced into the yard and shouted,

'Grand-dad, Grand-dad! I'm home!'

His Grand-dad came out of the house.

'Why so you are,' he said, 'And your face as red as a sunset too. What a runner you are!'

68

He gave Clive a hug and said, 'As soon as you've got your breath back, I've got something to show you, a little surprise.'
Clive liked surprises.
'Oh Grand-dad,' he said, 'What is it?'
'It's a little secret,' his Grand-dad said, 'You'll have to be very quiet. Come this way, now, as quiet as can be.'

Clive and his Grand-dad went very quietly into the dark barn. It was so dark that Clive couldn't see very well, but his Grand-dad took him by the hand and led him past the old tractor that lived there, right to a corner of the barn.

'There,' said Clive's Grand-dad, 'Do you see where I've made a little comfortable place with bales of hay, warm and quiet?'
But it was so dark Clive couldn't see anything.

'Never mind,' said his Grand-dad, 'In a while your eyes will get used to the darkness. You'll be able to see then.'
Clive looked hard and he listened for all he was worth. He heard tiny whimpering noises, and he didn't know what they could be. And then, as his eyes grew used to the darkness, he saw two bright eyes shining at him. It was Bess. She was lying on the hay and looking at Clive.
'It's Bess,' Clive whispered.
'Yes,' said his Grand-dad. 'It's lovely old Bess, my good old sheep-dog. Lie still, Bess, we shan't hurt them. She has something to show you, Clive.'
Then Clive knew what the secret was. 'It's puppies!' he said, 'She's got puppies!'
'Yes,' said his Grand-dad, 'Four of them. Four fine, fat puppies.'
'Can I pick them up, Grand-dad?' asked Clive.
'If you're gentle,' said his Grand-dad, 'and very careful.'
Clive's Grand-dad fondled Bess's head and ears. Very gently and carefully, Clive picked up the puppies one by one. They were warm and plump. Their eyes were closed, their noses black and shiny. They gave little sleepy cries, and when Clive put them down, they wriggled near their mother. Clive knew that they were beautiful.

'Can we keep them, Grand-dad?' he asked.
'Not all of them,' said his Grand-dad, 'We can't keep them all. Some of them will go to other farmers – I know that Mr Jenkins wants one. But we'll keep one of them. Which one shall it be?'
Clive looked at them all very carefully. They were all so pretty,

69

with white faces and paws and white tips to their tails. But one of them had small brown patches above his eyes, and a brown mark on one of his legs. Clive picked him up and showed him to his Grand-dad.

'It's this one, Grand-dad,' he said, 'We'll keep this little one with brown eye-brows.'

And they kept him. His name was Bob.

One day when Bob was only six weeks old, just a very small puppy, Clive and his Grand-dad were having tea in the kitchen. They heard a sudden fussing and clucking in the yard – it was the hens. They were bustling and running outside!

'What's the matter with those silly hens?' cried Grand-dad. Clive ran to the window and looked out. He began to laugh. 'Come quickly, Grand-dad,' he called, and his Grand-dad hurried over.

They saw tiny little Bob, rounding up all the hens in the yard. He crouched down, his little round stomach close to the ground, and he crept silently behind the fluttering hens, moving them together until they were all herded into a corner, against the wall. Then, his work finished, he sat down, his pink tongue hanging out, as if he were laughing. He thought he was a real sheepdog.

'Whee!' said Clive's Grand-dad, 'He's a proper little fellow, isn't he? You've picked a good dog for us there, Clive. I can see that he'll be very good with our sheep on the mountain, when he's big enough.' Clive said: 'Did you see him pretending that the hens were really sheep, Grand-dad? Did you see the way he herded them into the corner of the yard? Wasn't if fun to see him?'

'He is a good little dog,' said Grand-dad, 'now go and praise him, Clive, so that he will know he's done well.'

Clive was always kind and gentle to Bob. He watched him grow up to be a handsome sheepdog, strong and fast. He watched his Grand-dad train Bob on the mountain until Bob knew all his whistles and calls. Bob was a tireless runner, a stern guard, wise and obedient. He could round up the sheep and move them wherever they were to go. When Clive saw him running on the mountain, a black speck moving fast on the green grass, he felt proud. He knew that his Grand-dad could not keep his sheep without Bob's help. Bob could separate a sick sheep from the flock, and keep it there without moving until Clive's Grand-dad came with ointments and medicines to cure it. All day he worked on the hill, and at night he came down and lay by the fire at Clive's feet.

When Bob was three years old, a cold winter came. Shepherds have to know all about the weather, and Clive's Grand-dad was a very good shepherd. He could always tell what sort of day it would be. He had gone out in the morning and looked at the white frost covering the fields and looked up at the thick, black clouds hanging above the mountain, and he had shaken his head.

'What's the matter, Grand-dad?' Clive asked, just before he went to school.

'It looks like bad weather, Clive,' said Grand-dad, 'I don't like the look of those clouds at all, and it's so cold. I hope I'm wrong, but I think we are in for a spell of really bad weather. Hurry off to school now.'

All day in school, Clive felt the bitter cold, and when the bell rang for the end of lessons, he ran all the way home. His Grand-dad was in the yard, looking anxiously at the sky. He didn't smile when he saw Clive.

'Look at those ugly clouds,' he said to Clive, 'And feel the biting wind from the north. We shall have snow tonight, I can tell. Bob and I have brought down as many sheep as we can from the mountain, but a good many are still up there.'

Clive stared at the mountain. Great clouds covered the top and it was almost as dark as night. He was frightened for the sheep.

In bed that night Clive hoped that the snow would not fall, that their sheep would be safe on the mountain. But early the next morning his Grand-dad came and woke him up. It was not yet light and the lamp was lit in the kitchen.

'Eat your food quickly,' said Grand-dad, 'and dress in your warmest clothes. You and Bob must give me all the help you can today, or many of our sheep will die.'

Clive looked at his Grand-dad. He wore his great overcoat, his grey wool scarf, the hat with the flaps which covered his ears, his thick trousers, his high waterproof boots. Clive dressed quickly in all his warm clothes, and then his Grand-dad wrapped a clean sack about his shoulders.

They went into the yard. It was bitterly cold and the wind howled around the buildings. Heavy snow had fallen and the whole world seemed changed. Clive couldn't see the fences nor the pond.

The sheds and barns were covered by thick snow, the snow was as high as his Grand-dad's knees. And up in the mountains, where the snow was much deeper, the sheep were buried. They might die, unless they were found.

Clive and his Grand-dad started for the mountain. They carried long poles, to help them through the snow. Ahead of them they could see Bob bounding through the snowdrifts. They climbed higher, the snow above Clive's waist, but they found no sheep. They were very sad.

'How will I see them, Grand-dad,' called Clive, 'if they're buried under the snow?'

'I know how,' said Grand-dad. But then Bob suddenly barked. He lifted his head, barked once more, then pushed his nose into the snow.'

'Come on, Clive' shouted Grand-dad, 'Bob has found some of them. Good lad, Bob.'

They stumbled through the deep snow until they reached Bob.

There was nothing for Clive to see.

'Where are the sheep?' he asked.

His Grand-dad pushed his long pole through the snow until he felt the sheep deep beneath it.

'They're there,' he said, 'Bob's clever nose could smell them out, however deeply they're buried. And do you see this yellow stain on the top of the snow? That's where the warm breath of the sheep has climbed up through the snow. When you see that, you know the sheep are down there.'

He took his spade and began to dig for the lost sheep. Soon they bounded out and ran awkwardly away. They were all right. Now Grand-dad and Clive and Bob began to search for the rest of the flock, knowing they would all be nearby. Clive saw the yellow stains on the top of the snow, and dug the sheep out. Bob smelled the buried sheep under the snow. Grand-dad with his spade cleared the snow away so the sheep were free to run. And at the end of the day, all their sheep were saved. Bob drove them down into the big field near the house, so they would be safe through the bad weather.

'If it had not been for Bob,' Clive said to his Grand-dad 'We should have lost many of our sheep.'
'He is a good dog,' said his Grand-dad, 'I'm proud of him.'
Clive watched Bob as he slept near the fire.
'He is the best dog we've ever had,' Clive said, 'And he shall live with us all his life.'

And so he did.

Leslie Norris

Bob the Sheepdog

Bob was the dog I had when I was young,
  My friendly sheepdog, working on the hill.
I remember his kind eyes, his face, his lolling tongue
  I close my eyes, and I can see him still.

  Bob, come to the hill!
  We go to work the flock.
  Go bye, Bob! Down, lie still!
  Now take them gently past that craggy rock.
  Good boy, good sheepdog Bob.

Bob was the dog who helped us at our working
  When we were shepherds, when we kept our sheep,
Faithful, patient, clever, uncomplaining,
  Guarding the farm when we were fast asleep.

  Bob, come from the hill,
  The sheep are safe and warm.
  To heel, boy, come to heel,
  We'll walk home quietly to the welcoming farm.
  Good boy, good sheepdog Bob.

Leslie Norris.

The Shepherd's Friend

How can a shepherd work
   Without his dog?
How can he find his sheep
   In the freezing snow?
How can he drive them
   To fresh summer grass?
   Do you know?

The shepherd couldn't work
   Without his dog.
Without Bob, sheep would die
   In the winter snow.
Nor could the shepherd guard
   All his white lambs.
   That much I know.

Leslie Norris

Vic the Sheepdog

Look, see them running
   Over the hill!
They're Farmer Jenkins' sheep
   And they won't keep still.

They've kicked up their feet
   And jumped over the wall,
Soon there will be none of them
   Left at all!

But here comes Vic
   In his coat white and black,
And he's racing and racing
   To chase them back.

He's Farmer Jenkins' sheepdog,
   Clever and quick –
He's brought them all back again!
   Well done, Vic!

Leslie Norris

The Shepherd and His Dog

They be climbing up the hill,
All our sheep, all our sheep,
For the morning air be chill,
And the fields they lie still,
And the wordle be asleep,
Say the Shepherd and his dog.

Now the sun be all aglow,
All our sheep, all our sheep.
They do take their way below,
Where the little streams do go,
And the sweetest of keep,
Say the Shepherd and his dog.

Now we bring them whoame to fold,
All our sheep, all our sheep,
For the moon be rising gold,
And the evening air blows cold,
Down over the steep,
Say the Shepherd and his dog.

Oh the lambs be coming too,
All our sheep, all our sheep,
Trittle-trotting by each ewe,
Every fleece adrench with dew,
All our pretty, pretty sheep,
Say the Shepherd and his dog.

Composed and sung by 'Old Shepherd',
Blackdown Hills, 1870-1903,
collected by Ruth Tongue.

wordle – *world*
whoame – *home*

David and the Giant

David lay on a hilltop under the warm sun and listened to the peaceful sound of his sheep chomping the grass. David was a shepherd boy and it was his job to look after the sheep and see that no harm came to them. Beside him on the grass lay his shepherd's crook and his harp. David loved to play music and make songs, but on a hot day like this even his harp seemed sleepy, as if it just wanted to lie still.

'David! David!'
David sat up, wide awake. It was his father's voice calling to him. All David's family were shepherds, but David's older brothers had gone away to fight in a war. David was only thirteen and too young to go. His father sounded anxious:
'David, where are you?'
'Here, Father.'
David's father came running up the hill, puffing and gasping for breath, and dropped down beside him on the grass.
'What's the matter, Father?' asked David. 'It isn't bad news about the war is it? Are my brothers all right? Nothing's happened to them, has it?'
'No, no, my boy,' said his father, getting his breath back. 'Nothing's wrong. Well, when I say nothing's wrong, nothing's right either.'
'What do you mean, Father?'
'When I say nothing's wrong I mean your brothers are all right. They haven't been hurt in the fighting. But when I say nothing's right I mean that the war is still going on, and it's getting worse. Our enemies, the Philistines, are getting stronger. And our King's army is getting weaker. Soon there'll be another battle, and if the Philistines win what will happen to us, and to our farms and our homes?'
'But we have brave soldiers,' said David.
'And the Philistines have Goliath,' said his father.
'Who's Goliath?'
'Goliath is a giant.'

'Oh, Father!' said David. 'I don't believe in giants!'
'Well,' said his father, 'you'd believe in Goliath if you saw him.
He's ten feet tall. His voice is like thunder. His spear is like a tree
trunk. And as for his sword – it's as tall as you are. All our men are
afraid to fight him. He's as fierce as a wild beast.'

David didn't say any more but he thought to himself:
'I know how to deal with a wild beast.' And he did too, because
sometimes a wolf or a bear or a lion would come out of the hills to
attack his sheep. If a sheep strayed away from the flock, or if one
was sick or if there were new born lambs they were likely to be
caught. David had to be very watchful, and he had a weapon that
would drive away a wolf or a lion even from a distance. This was a
sling; a strap of leather into which David fitted a stone. Then he
took the two ends of the strap, and whirled it round his head –
faster and faster he whirled it – and then he let one end of the strap
go so that the stone sped straight to its mark. David could send a
shower of stones to hit any wild animal that came to attack his
sheep until, however, hungry it was, it ran away snarling.

But now his father had something special for him to do.
'I want you to go to the King's camp,' he said, 'and take some food
to your brothers. I'll look after the sheep.'

So David set off to find his brothers. He wondered if he would see
the King. And if he did, would the King remember him? Because
once David had played his harp to the King when he was ill and
the music had made the King feel better.

After walking for a long time David saw the smoke of camp-fires
rising above the trees, and heard men's voices and the clatter of
weapons. A soldier stepped out in front of him and asked him who
he was and what he wanted. When David told him, the soldier took
him through a little wood and into the King's camp

The tents of the King's soldiers were pitched on a hill, on one side
of a valley. At the bottom of the valley was a small stream, and on
the hill on the other side was the army of the Philistines. Their
camp was much larger, their tents covered the hillside; their flags
fluttered in the wind, and their spears glittered in the sunshine.
'Look there!' said the soldier to David.
But David did not need to be told to look. On the hill across the
valley, outside the biggest of the tents in the Philistine camp, stood
the giant.

'That's Goliath!' said the soldier. 'His voice is like thunder, his spear is like a tree trunk, and his sword is twice as tall as you are.'

Standing up there on the hillside, with all his armour shining in the sun, and his plumed helmet on his head, the giant looked even bigger than anyone said he was, and when he shouted his voice echoed across the valley like thunder so that all the men in the King's army heard it.

'Come on, come and fight me!' he bellowed. 'Come and fight Goliath. Why don't you come? Are you scared?'

'Yes, we are,' muttered the soldier to David. 'Not even our bravest soldiers dare to fight him. Even the King dare not.'

'I will fight him' said David.

'Stop!' shouted the soldier. 'You mustn't go that way.'

But David ran away from him. He ran into the middle of the camp where he could see the King's tent. Before anyone could stop him he pushed inside, and kneeling at the King's feet he said:

'I will go and fight Goliath.'

The King stared at him for a moment in surprise. Then he threw back his head and roared with laughter. And the soldiers that were with him laughed too.

'Fight Goliath!' exclaimed the King. 'But you're only a boy. My bravest soldiers dare not fight Goliath.'

'And the King doesn't dare!' whispered David to himself.

The King stopped laughing. He frowned. 'What's that you say?'

'I said – I said – I haven't anything to wear.'

'Oh – you want armour to wear, do you?' said the King, laughing again. 'You want to look like a soldier. Very well, my boy. You shall have *my* armour. Then we'll see if you still think you can fight Goliath.'

The King told his soldiers to bring his own splendid shining armour and put it on David. They buckled on leg pieces of heavy metal that reached above his knees so that he could hardly walk, they fastened a breast-plate across his chest that was so heavy he could hardly breathe, they gave him arm-pieces that came nearly to his shoulders and prevented him from bending his elbows, and last of all they put a helmet on his head that was so large it came right down over his eyebrows so that he couldn't see a thing.

'Now you look like a soldier!' cried the King. 'Quick march! Left, right! Left, right!'

78

David took a step forward, stumbled and fell flat on his face with a deafening clatter. The King and his soldiers bellowed with laughter.

David tore off the helmet and threw it on the floor, he struggled out of the armour piece by piece and threw each piece as far away from him as he could. He said to the King: 'I *will* fight Goliath. Nothing will stop me now. But I'll do it with my own weapons. I'm a shepherd and I've often driven a wild beast away from my flock. Now I'll drive this giant away from my people in the same way. I'm going now. But can I leave my harp here with you, so that it will be safe?'

The King had stopped laughing. He looked at David kindly. 'I remember you now,' he said. 'You're the boy who played to me when I was ill and made me better. What's your name?'
'David, Your Majesty.'
'David,' said the King, 'don't be angry because we laughed at you. I don't want you to be hurt. Go home and take care of your sheep. Come back and play some more of your songs to me one day when the war is over. Forget about fighting Goliath. You can't. He really is a giant. He's ten feet all. His voice is like thunder. His spear is like a tree trunk. And his sword is three times as tall as you are.'
'Well, I don't care if it's ten times as tall,' said David. 'The Lord God will take care of me. I'm going to stop him killing my people.'

The King called to him to come back, but David dodged past the soldiers, who tried to stop him, and darted out of the tent. He ran through the camp and down the hill, and crawled along the valley, hidden by rocks, to the edge of the little stream. The water was shallow and rippled over smooth round pebbles. David slid his hand into the water and picked up five stones. Then he jumped over the stream and shouted at the top of his voice:
'Hey, you ugly monster! Can you hear me, you great galumphing Goliath?'

Goliath had been looking across the valley at the soldiers.
He hadn't noticed a boy crawling along by the stream.
Now he turned his head and looked down.
'What's that squeaking down there?' he growled.
'I'm over here, onion head!' shouted David.
Goliath saw him, and like the King he laughed. His laughter rumbled like thunder.

'What are you?' he bellowed. ' A mouse? A little squeaking mouse? Or could it be a boy? A little boy with a stick. Little boy, do you think you've come after a dog with a stick?'

David called back: 'You have a sword as tall as me and a spear like a tree trunk. But I'm not afraid. I have the Lord God to take care of me.'

Goliath laughed even louder. He banged his sword on his shield and shouted:

'I am Goliath!'

David took his sling from his belt.

'I am ten feet tall!'

David fitted one of the stones into the sling.

'My voice is like thunder!'

David whirled the sling round his head. He whirled it faster and faster. He let it go and the stone sped straight to Goliath. It struck him on the forehead. And the giant fell, he crashed to the ground and lay still . . .

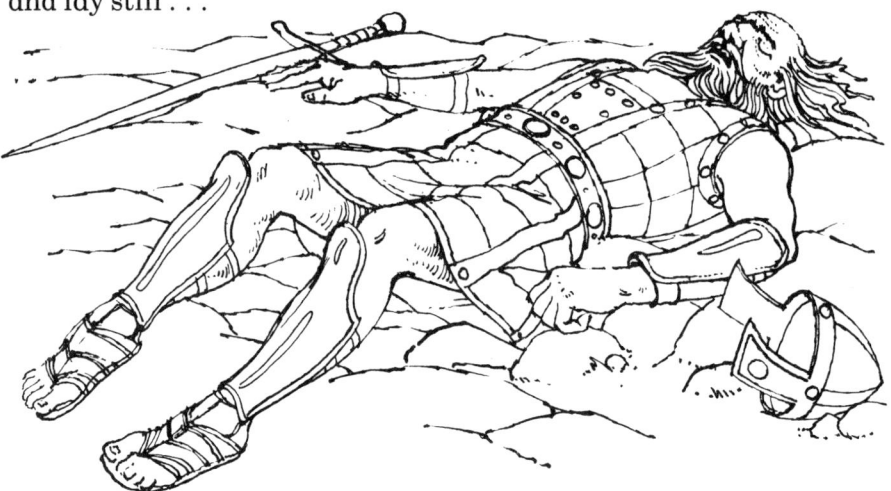

Goliath the giant was dead. David the shepherd was back at home with his sheep. Once more he could stretch out on the grass, and feel the warm sun on his face and listen to his sheep peacefully chomping. Now he knew that his people were safe, their fields and their homes were safe, because a shepherd boy had not been afraid of a giant. David thought:

'Perhaps I could make a song about it.'

He picked up his harp and began to play.

Geoffrey Curtis

80

David's Shepherd's Song

The sheep on the hillside
And sheep by the stream
Are peacefully grazing
Where bright waters gleam.

But sheep in the valley
Are trembling with fright
Surrounded by wolves
In the darkness of night.

The shepherd comes running
He's ready to fight
His sling-stone goes flying
Wolves vanish from sight.

Now safe in their sheep fold
The flock will not roam,
But where can the shepherd
Find safety, find home?

For I am the shepherd
Who fights for his sheep,
But who protects me
Awake or asleep?

The Lord God of Hosts
Is my shepherd I know
He brings me to meadows
Where calm waters flow.

Geoffrey Curtis

Michael's Lamb

Michael lived with his father and mother at a lonely farm high up in the hills. In summertime, the sheep from the farm wandered all over the hills eating the green grass. But now it was winter. The grass was covered in deep snow and the wind was icy cold. Michael couldn't go down the hill to his school in the village because the snow was too deep.

When the snow first began to fall, Michael's father took his sheepdog, Meg, up into the hills. They collected all the sheep and brought them down to the farm so that they would be safe until the snow melted. Michael's father put the sheep that were soon going to have their lambs into pens near the farmhouse so that he could take special care of them. Every morning and every night they had to be fed. Michael liked helping with this job.

One night, after tea, when it was already dark and more snow was falling, Michael took his torch and went out to feed the sheep. As they came to the end of the pen to eat the food, Michael counted them – one, two, three, four, five, six, seven, eight, nine – Nine? He was sure there should be ten! He looked round with his torch but that was all he could see. If a sheep had got out of the pen it might be hurt, or lost. Michael ran back to the farmhouse, and burst into the warm kitchen where his mother and father were sitting with Meg the dog lying at their feet.
'Dad, Dad!' cried Michael, 'How many sheep should there be in the pen nearest the barn?'
'Ten,' said his father. 'Why?'
'Well, I think there are only nine,' said Michael. 'But I couldn't see very well in the dark. They were making a lot of noise, too, as if something had frightened them.'
'You'd better go and have a look yourself, Dad,' said Michael's mother, and she brought his father's coat out of the hall and another torch.
'You didn't let one out while you were feeding them did you?' said his father.

'No,' said Michael, 'they were all at the other side of the pen, huddled together, against the barn wall, out of the wind.'
'Well, we'd best go and see,' said his father. Meg, the dog, jumped up too, waving her tail. She knew something was wrong. 'Come on, lass,' said the farmer, 'we'll need you.'

Michael opened the door, and the cold wind blew snow in their faces as they ran across the farmyard to the pen. They knew that they must hurry. If a sheep was lost, and her lamb was born in the cold and snow, both she and her baby might die. Meg the dog, trotted in front of them. With her bright eyes and keen nose, she would help them to find the sheep.
Meg sniffed all round the pen while they counted the sheep again – one, two, three, four, five, six, seven, eight, nine – yes, there was one missing.

Michael called out, 'Look, Dad, look! I've found a gap in the fence – that's where she must have got out.'
His father went to look. 'Yes, that's it,' he said. 'But I can't see any tracks. The snow must have covered them up. Come on, Meg, come on, lass! You'll have to help us find her. Sniff her out, Meg – seek and find!'

Meg sniffed along the fence. She could smell where the sheep had gone. She ran fast over the snow, sniffing all the time. Michael followed her, keeping the torch-light on her so that he would not lose her in the dark. Suddenly she stopped and began to bark.

They ran over to her. Meg was standing beside a ditch. It had been hidden under the snow, and the lost sheep had fallen into it. She was lying on her side at the bottom of the ditch.
'Daft old thing!' said Michael's father. 'Let's try to get her up.'

They bent down to lift the sheep, but then Michael's father said quickly: 'No, no, leave her Michael. Her lamb is going to be born. We can't move her now. Run and tell your mother to bring water and a piece of towelling, and fetch me a bale of straw from the barn.'

Michael ran as fast as he could to the farmhouse and told his mother what had happened. She scrambled into a coat, and found the old towel his father wanted. Then she and Michael carried a bucket of water and the bale of straw from the barn back to where the farmer was waiting. They put the bale of straw beside the sheep to shelter her from the cold wind and scattered some loose straw behind her in the ditch. 'Do you need any more help?' asked Michael's mother.

'No thanks, love,' said his Dad. 'You go back to the house and put the kettle on. We shall need a hot drink when we come in.'

Michael and his father crouched down in the snow. They held their torches up over the sheep and waited. The farmer talked gently to the sheep so that she wouldn't be afraid:

'Now then, old lass,' he said, 'you'll be all right.'

Suddenly Michael said: 'Look, Dad, look, I can see the lamb's head.' In a few seconds a tiny baby lamb lay, bleating softly, on the straw. 'It's a very tiny one,' said Michael. 'Poor little thing. It's shaking with the cold. Will it be all right?'

'I don't know,' said his father. 'It's very small. We'd better look sharp and get it inside in the warm. We'll just get the mother to lick it clean. Come on, old lass.'

Michael's father held the tiny new born lamb in front of its mother's nose, so that she could smell the lamb and lick it clean and dry with her warm rough tongue. Then Michael and Meg took the mother sheep back to the pen. The farmer gently wrapped the old towel round the shivering lamb and ran with it to the farmhouse. He carried the lamb into the warm kitchen, where Michael's mother was waiting anxiously.

'Is it all right?' she said.

'No, it's a very tiny one,' said the farmer. 'We'll have to be quick if we're going to save it.'

'Give it to me,' said Michael's mother. 'You make a bottle of milk for it. The powder's in the larder and the medicine's in the fridge.'

Michael came in and his mother sent him running upstairs to fetch an old blanket. Then they all knelt down together on the rug beside the fire with the lamb. Michael rubbed it gently with the towel and his mother tried to get it to drink a few drops of milk from a baby's feeding bottle. At first the lamb was too weak. Michael began to feel anxious.

'It's not feeding,' he said. 'Is it going to die?'

His mother said: 'It will be all right, if it drinks this.'

'It won't open it's mouth,' said Michael. 'It's not moving at all.'

'It's shocked and frightened that's all,' said his mother. 'Keep on rubbing it gently, Michael, keep it warm.'

His father said: 'Give it taste of the milk. Open its mouth and force a drop or two inside.'

84

'All right,' said his mother, 'take hold of the bottle, Michael, while I open its mouth. Now when I say squeeze, squeeze – mind you, don't squeeze too much.'

Carefully, Michael did as his mother told him. Some drops of milk were squeezed into the lamb's mouth.
'It's still not moving,' said Michael.
'Give it time,' said his father.
'Come on, little 'un,' said his mother, softly. And then, suddenly, Michael saw the lamb move its head, and they heard a tiny bleating sound.
'It's tasted the milk,' said Michael's mother.
'It's drinking! It's drinking!' cried Michael.
The lamb bleated again and slowly began to suck the warm milk from the bottle.
'It will be all right now,' said his father.

They watched as the lamb drank the milk, and its sucking and bleating got stronger and stronger. Then they wrapped it warmly in the old blanket and put it in the box beside the fire. Meg the dog lay down contentedly beside the box. Michael and his mother and father all had a hot drink before they went to bed.

After that, in the next few days, several more lambs were born on the farm. Michael's lamb grew big and strong and went to play with the others in the pen. They would all have looked alike to you and me, but Michael always knew which one was his special lamb.

Timothy Wilkinson

Christmas Presents

Do you like to give presents?
People gave Jesus presents when he was born.
Now we give each other presents on his birthday.

The Boy and His Drum

On a cold winter night, long long ago, two people came to a little town where the houses were shut up, and dark.
Mary was riding on a shaggy brown donkey, and Joseph was walking beside the donkey, leading it along through the cold, dark streets, searching for somewhere to sleep.

It seemed that there was nowhere, no room for them anywhere, nowhere to rest in this little town of Bethlehem. Then, at last, they found a warm shelter. A woman let them sleep in a stable, where animals slept. It was warm and dry. There was straw to lie down on. During the night, Mary's baby was born.

When morning came, the first Christmas morning, light shone in through the open door on to Mary and Joseph and the new born baby. The shaggy brown donkey was there, too, resting after his long journey. In a corner, some cows were lying, contented. And high in the rafters perched two grey doves.

Mary smiled down at the new born baby held gently in her arms, and sang softly to him.
'Lullay my dear son, my own one, my liking,
Lullay my dear one, my own dear darling.'
Then the light shining in from the doorway darkened. There were men at the doorway looking in.
Mary held her baby more closely, but Joseph came to stand beside her and put a comforting hand on her shoulder. There was no need to worry. The men were shepherds. Last night on the hills outside the town they'd been looking after their flocks of sheep. Then they'd heard that the baby was going to be born, and they'd come and searched for him.

Mary smiled. She beckoned the shepherds into the stable, and they smiled too when they saw the baby. They came in, quietly, and knelt before him.
Mary looked down at the gentle shepherds. So quiet, she thought, so very careful not to frighten her baby. Of course, they had never looked after a new born baby, but they'd often looked after a new

born lamb. They'd often cared for a new born lamb just as gently as Mary cared for her baby.

They'd brought a gift of a warm woollen blanket for Mary to wrap around the baby. Was it one of the sheep that gave the wool?

The shepherds looked around the stable. They saw the shaggy grey donkey, and the cows, and the two grey doves in the rafters. Such a rough place, they thought, for the baby to be born. Just a stable, where animals sleep.

The donkey, and the cows, and the two grey doves looked back at the shepherds as if they tried to say, 'We did what we could. We all tried to help.'

The donkey shook his ears: 'I carried his mother. I brought her here safely to Bethlehem.'

A brown and white cow looked up and seemed to say: 'I gave him my manger for a bed to lie in. I gave him my hay, for a pillow for his head.'

The doves in the rafters fluttered their wings: 'We cooed him to sleep, so he wouldn't cry.'

The friendly beasts had done all they could for Jesus, the new born baby. They were the first to know about the baby.

But before very long, many people knew. And they wanted to come to the stable and see him, and bring him gifts on this first Christmas day.

One of these people coming to the stable was a boy who had nothing to give to the baby. The boy had no money, or anything to give.

The only thing he had was a drum, which he played:

Parum pum pum pum, as he walked along. *Parum pumpum pum,* as he came to the stable.

Parum pum pum pum.

But what use was a drum to a new born baby? Unless . . . of course! Could he play for the baby?

The boy looked in through the stable door. Was it all right if he played for the baby? Would Mary be pleased? Would the baby smile? Mary looked up. She nodded her head.

Then the boy played his drum. He played his best:

Parum pum pum pum. Parum pum pum pum.

Parum pum pum pum.

And the baby smiled at the boy and his drum.

Anita Hewett
88

The Little Drummer boy *Come They Told Me*

Come, they told, me,
> *parum pum pum pum –*

A new-born King to see,
> *parum pum pum pum –*

Our finest gifts we bring
> *parum pum pum pum –*

To lay before the King,
> *parum pum pum pum*
> *rum pum pum pum rum pum pum pum*

So to honour him,
> *parum pum pum pum –*

When we come.

Little baby
> *parum pum pum pum –*

I am a poor boy too
> *parum pum pum pum –*

I have no gift to bring
> *parum pum pum pum –*

That's fit to give our King
> *parum pum pum pum –*
> *rum pum pum pum rum pum pum pum*

Shall I play for you
> *parum pum pum pum –*

On my drum?

Mary nodded
> *parum pum pum pum*

The ox and ass kept time
> *parum pum pum pum*

I played my drum for him
> *parum pum pum pum*

I played my best for him
> *parum pum pum pum*
> *rum pum pum pum rum pum pum pum*

Then he smiled at me
> *parum pum pum pum*

Me and my drum.

Katherine Wood

The Cherry Tree Carol

Mary and Joseph
Their substance was small
They could get no lodging
In the city at all.

Mary and Joseph
In a stable did hie
With oxen and asses they
Used for to lie.

Mary and Joseph
They thought it no harm
And before the next morning
Our Saviour was born.

Mary dressed her baby
And she dressed it so neat
And in an old manger
She laid it to sleep.

from The Cherry Tree Carol, Anon

As Dew in April

He came all so still
Where his mother was
As dew in April
That falleth on the grass.

He came all so still
To his mother's bower
As dew in April
That falleth on the flower.

He came all so still
Where his mother lay
As dew in April
That falleth on the spray.

from As Dew in April, Anon

The Star of the Nativity

It was winter . . .
The wind blew . . .
It was cold for the Child
In the cave on the hillside.
He was warmed by the breath of an ox
The farm animals
Were stabled in the cave
And a warm haze drifted over the manger.

from 'The Star of the Nativity'
by Boris Pasternak
translated by Max Hayward and Manya Harari

Baboushka

Once upon a time, long ago in a far-off country called Russia, there lived an old woman. She was called Baboushka. Baboushka lived all alone in a little house in the middle of a forest.

One cold winter's night the snow lay deep on the ground, and an icy wind blew through the trees. But Baboushka was snug and warm inside her little house. She was sitting in front of a cheerful log-fire, having a little sleep after her evening meal. Suddenly there came a loud knocking at the door. It made Baboushka jump. Then a voice called out:
'Baboushka! Baboushka! Let us in.'
'Who is it?' said the old woman, 'What do you want?'
'We're travellers who need to shelter from the snow,' said the voice. Baboushka went and opened the door, and the icy wind made her shiver.
Outside in the snow, stood three tall men, dressed in long fur robes. They looked like princes. Baboushka was so surprised at first, that she only stood and stared at them. Then she saw how cold and tired they looked.
'Come in, come in, gentlemen' she said. 'Welcome to my little house. You must be freezing. Come and warm yourselves by the fire.'
The three men came in, and shut the door.
'That's it. Now take off your wet coats, and come to the fire.'

The three men took off their long fur coats, and gathered round the fire. Baboushka's little house had never been so full.
'I'll put some soup on the stove to heat', said the old woman.
'I expect you could do with it.' And she began to bustle about, preparing things.
'Oh dear, I'm afraid I haven't much to give you. And my house is too small to offer much comfort to such fine gentlemen. Tell me, who are you? Are you princes?'
92

The eldest man smiled at her and said:

'No Baboushka, we are not princes. We are three wise men from the east. We study the stars. My name is Balthasar, and my two friends here are called Caspar and Melchior.'

The other two men bowed to Baboushka.

'Well, Balthasar, Caspar and Melchior', said Baboushka, 'You are very welcome in my house. But, tell me – where are you going on such a cold winter's night as this?'

'We are following a star', said Melchior, 'a star that will lead us to the Prince of Peace.'

Baboushka looked puzzled. 'The Prince of Peace', she said, 'Who is that?'

'The Baby Jesus', said Caspar, 'We are taking presents to give to him.'

Then the three wise men showed Baboushka the presents they were taking to the Baby Jesus. Balthasar's present was a box of gold coins. Caspar's was frankincense, which had a beautiful smell. And Melchior's present was myrrh, a precious ointment which takes away pain. Baboushka had never seen such splendid presents.

'How wonderful', she said. 'Thank you for showing them to me. But tell me, do you know where the star will lead you?'

'A long, long way', said Balthasar, 'into another country.'

Baboushka sighed. 'Oh, how I wish I could see the Prince of Peace, the Baby Jesus.'

'Why not come with us?' said Caspar.

Baboushka could hardly believe her ears.

'Oh no, no', she said, 'I'm too old to go on such a long journey, especially in weather like this. No, it's out of the question. Now, come along, your soup's ready. Sit down at the table, all of you.'

After supper, the three wise men stayed and rested in Baboushka's little house, and by the next evening it had stopped snowing, and the stars were shining again in a clear, cold sky. It was time for the three wise men to go on their journey. Balthasar tried once more to persuade Baboushka to come with them.

'Please change your mind', he said. 'We'll take care of you.'

'But I haven't a present for the Baby', said Baboushka, 'I've nothing good enough to bring to the Prince of Peace.'

'You don't need a present,' said Melchior, 'just bring yourself.'

For a moment Baboushka looked undecided, then she said:
'No. I can't leave my little house, and all the things I have
to do here.'
'That's a great pity', said Caspar sadly, 'Well, thank you for all
your kindness, Baboushka. Now we must be on our way. Goodbye.'
'Goodbye to you, gentlemen', said Baboushka. 'A safe journey
to you.'

When the three wise men had gone, Baboushka settled herself
comfortably once more, in front of her fire. Then she began
muttering to herself.
'I wonder how they knew my name? They were fine gentlemen.
And their presents for the Prince of Peace were really wonderful.
But a baby wouldn't want such precious things, he'd want toys to
play with. Yes, of course he would. Now, I wonder if I could find
something for him.'

Baboushka got up, and shuffled across to a big, wooden cupboard
in a corner of the room. After searching around for a while, she found
a red ball, some brightly-painted wooden beads, and a rattle. 'There
we are', she said. 'These are just the right sort of things for a little
baby to play with. Now, where's my basket? I must go after the
three wise men, and catch them up. Where's my shawl? I must hurry!'
And Baboushka quickly put on her shawl, fetched her basket from
the cupboard, put the toys carefully in the basket, and went out
into the cold, crisp night, banging her little front door behind her.
'Caspar, Melchior, Balthasar', she called, 'Wait for me!
Where are you?'

But there was no reply, only the sound of the wind whistling in the
trees. On and on Baboushka went, trudging through the snow. She
asked everyone she met if they knew which way the three wise
men had gone, but no one had seen them. She never caught up
with them. She searched and searched for the place where the
Prince of Peace was born, but she never found him.

Some people say that Baboushka never stopped searching, that she
is wandering and looking for him still. But sometimes, at Christmas,
she stops at houses where little children live. Old Baboushka
comes when the children are asleep, and from her basket she leaves
her brightly-painted wooden toys beside their beds.

A Russian legend re-told by Clifford Norgate
94

Baboushka's Carol

Hear on the wind,
Calling from far away,
Lost in the night,
Wand'ring through the day,
A voice from the past
Searches from year to year,
Where is the King?
Is the new baby here?

'If only I had not stayed behind,
If only I'd gone the new King to find.'

How can we tell
What it was like to see,
That tiny child
Born for you and me?
For only a few
Shepherds were there to know
How three wise men
Found him so long ago.

If only we could have been there too,
If only we knew what three wise men knew.

'Wait for me now,'
Whispers that voice of old,
'Show me the way,
I bring him toys to hold.'
Baboushka will place
Toys on your pillow too
Gifts for a king
Born a child just like you.

If only I could have been there too,
If only I knew what three wise men knew.

Sarah McNeill

Jacqui's Gift

It was nearly Christmas. All the children at Jacqui's school had been thinking about it and getting ready for it.

Some of them had written letters to Father Christmas. At home their mothers were busy making Christmas cakes and puddings. At school they were making decorations for their classroom, getting ready for the Christmas play and talking about parties. Jacqui's teacher told them the story of the first Christmas when Jesus was born in the stable in Bethlehem. She told them about the shepherds who had heard about the special baby and had come to see him in the manger.

The bit of the story Jacqui liked best was the part about the three wise men who travelled so far to bring their gifts to the new baby. When the teacher told them this part of the story she said: 'We can't give our presents to Baby Jesus on his birthday, but we can give them to other people.'

When Jacqui got home from school she found Daddy in the kitchen making tea. When she had taken off her coat and put on her slippers, she went into the kitchen to help. She could hear her Mummy upstairs with her baby brother Matthew.

While she helped Daddy to get tea ready Jacqui told him about the cards they were going to make next day at school. Daddy said, 'Have you decided what you're going to put on your card?'
'I think I'll put a Christmas tree on it. I like drawing them,' said Jacqui.
'I expect lots of people will draw Christmas trees,' said Daddy. 'Can't you think of something else?'
Jacqui thought for a moment or two. 'I suppose I could draw a snowman,' she said.
'That's a good idea,' said Daddy. 'Perhaps you could draw some children making the snowman as well.'
'Yes, that'll be good,' said Jacqui. 'I could draw Claire and me.'

'That sounds lovely,' said Daddy. 'Here you are, take the plate of cakes and put it on the table and then tea is about ready.'

Jacqui carried the plate of cakes into the next room. She saw that Daddy had forgotten the spoon for the jam, so she went back into the kitchen again. Daddy was filling the teapot with hot water to make the tea.
'Daddy,' she said, 'Sophie says she's going to buy her Daddy a present for Christmas. Can I buy you something?'
'That's a lovely idea,' said Daddy. 'But why don't you buy Mummy something, as a surprise? Keep it a secret. She'd love that. And you could give her your Christmas card as well.'
'But I haven't got much money,' said Jacqui. 'Sophie's got older brothers and sisters and they are all joining their pocket money together to buy something.'
'Well you can buy something small, but something Mummy really likes,' said Daddy. 'We shall have to think hard.'
They heard Mummy coming downstairs with Baby Matthew to have tea, so Daddy said quickly, 'We'll go out on Saturday morning shall we and see what we can buy? You must keep it a secret though, then it will be a real surprise.'

When Saturday came Daddy wakened Jacqui quite early with a drink of orange juice. He spoke very softly so that Mummy wouldn't hear what he was saying. 'Shall we go shopping today for that secret present?' he said.
'Ooh, yes please,' said Jacqui. 'What shall I buy her?'
'Let's see how much money you've got in your money box,' said Daddy.

They tipped the coins out of her piggy bank on to the bed, and counted them up.

'What do you think I could get with this, it isn't very much is it?' said Jacqui. She wished she had lots more money in her piggy bank for present buying.
'I think you'll be able to buy something nice with that amount,' said Daddy. 'We'll go into town this morning and see shall we? Did you make your Christmas card at school?'
'Yes, it's here in my reading book,' said Jacqui.
'That's lovely!' said Daddy. Jacqui had drawn the snowman and given him a black hat and red scarf and an orange carroty nose. She had drawn herself and Claire wearing their bright woolly hats

and scarves and gloves. It looked very gay. 'Mummy will love that,' said Daddy. 'Quick hide it away in your drawer, I can hear Mummy coming.'

After breakfast Mummy said: 'What are you going to do this morning Jacqui?'
'I'm going shopping with Daddy,' Jacqui said.
'Oh, are you?' said her Mummy. 'I thought you were going to play with Claire.'
'Jacqui's going to help me choose some decorations for the Christmas tree,' said Daddy, and he smiled a secret smile at Jacqui. Jacqui smiled another secret smile back at Daddy. She liked the feeling that they had a special job to do together without Mummy or Baby Matthew knowing about it.

After breakfast Daddy and Jacqui set off to the shops. They all looked very gay and Christmassy. Many of them had Christmas trees in their windows and others had windows full of Christmas presents. Jacqui looked at a lot of them. There were lots of lovely things that she was sure Mummy would like but they all cost a lot more than she had to spend.

At last they came to the newspaper shop. Daddy always called there to pay for their newspapers and magazines. Jacqui went in with him. She knew Mr Wilson who owned the shop very well. As well as newspapers, he sold sweets and pencils and some cards and games.
'Hullo Jacqui,' he said. 'Are you shopping with Daddy today?'
'Yes,' said Jacqui. 'I'm going to buy Mummy a Christmas present.'
Mr Wilson smiled. 'Your Mummy likes sweets doesn't she? Were you thinking of getting her some?'
Jacqui hadn't thought of it, but it did seem like a good idea.
Lots of packets of sweets and chocolates had special Christmas wrappings on.
'What do you think Jacqui?' said Daddy.
'She likes milk chocolate, doesn't she?' said Jacqui. 'Yes, I think that's what I'll get.'
She looked carefully at all the different bars of chocolate and at last she chose one she knew Mummy would like. It had nuts and fruit in it.
'I'll have that one please,' she said.
Mr Wilson wrapped the chocolate in a brown paper bag.

'We'd better find some Christmas wrapping paper for you,'
said Daddy.
They chose a pretty red paper with holly leaves and Christmas
bells on it, and then they left the shop together and went home
again.

Jacqui wrapped up the bar of chocolate in the wrapping paper and
stuck it down tightly with sticky tape. She put her Christmas card
in an envelope and wrote on the outside: 'To Mummy with love
from Jacqui'. Then she hid the parcel in her bedroom and kept it a
secret.

On Christmas morning Jacqui woke early. Father Christmas had
filled her stocking and brought her a paint box, and a landrover
and trailer with a horse inside and a book. He'd brought Matthew
a boat to sail in the bath, a ball and a picture book. When Jacqui
went downstairs there was a big pile of exciting-looking presents
under the Christmas tree. Mummy said they would open them
after breakfast. Jacqui had her present for Mummy hidden inside
her jumper; she put it amongst the others under the tree without
Mummy seeing.

Nobody wanted much to eat for breakfast. At last when breakfast
was cleared away Jacqui said 'Can we open the presents round the
tree now?'

They all gathered round the tree.
'What a wonderful pile of presents,' said Mummy.
Daddy picked the top one off the pile. 'To Jacqui from Grandpa.'
he said. Jacqui opened the parcel excitedly.
'Oh a leggo set!' she said.
'Here's one for Daddy from Grandma,' said Mummy. There were
socks in that one.

It seemed to Jacqui that Mummy would never find her present. It
was hiding there underneath some of the others. She wished
Mummy would notice it.
Daddy said: 'Oh, Mummy, look at this one. There's a card with it –
oh, it says from Jacqui to Mummy. It's long and flat. I wonder what
it is!'
'Open it, open it, Mummy!' cried Jacqui.
'What a lovely snowman card!' said Mummy. 'Did you make it?'
'Yes, yes I did,' said Jacqui.

'It's very pretty!' said Mummy. 'And what's this?'
She tore off the pretty Christmas paper. 'Oh!' she said and she smiled her happiest smile. 'Oh, my favourite chocolate! Oh thank you darling! You are a kind little girl.'
'Was it a real surprise, Mummy?' asked Jacqui.
'Yes it was!' said Mummy.
'Did you know I was going to give you a present?'
'No, I didn't,' said Mummy.
'It was hard to keep the secret,' said Jacqui.
'I'm sure it was,' said Mummy.
'But it was worth it, wasn't it?' said Daddy.
'Yes, I like making surprises for people,' said Jacqui.

She felt so happy about her lovely surprise and so glad Daddy had suggested it.
'Next year I'll do it *all* by myself,' she decided.
'That's the fun of Christmas,' said Daddy. 'Making surprises and making people happy. Happy Christmas everybody!'

Timothy and Pat Wilkinson

The Music

Some of the poems in this book are songs too. The tunes and accompaniments of these are printed in the following pages.

Blackbird's Song

1 Ba - by black-birds come from eggs And ba - by black-birds grow,—
2 From those eggs new black-birds come, And then those black-birds grow,—

When they've grown, they lay more eggs, As— ev - 'ry - one should know.—
When they've grown, they lay more eggs, It— al - ways will be so.——

To sing this as a round, the second voice begins
when the first voice has reached the figure 2.

It's Not Much Fun

1 It's not much fun when you're play-ing on your own. No it's

not much fun if you're play-ing all a - lone. You can

race your-self and chase your-self, and drive your-self a-round, You can

hide your-self and slide your-self and push you to the ground, You can

tell your-self a stor - y, a po - em or a song, But it's

not much fun to have to play on your own for long.

Hello's a Handy Word

Talking

New Things To Do

New things to do, New plac-es to go, New things to learn, New peo-ple to know, New things to see New things to hear, We'll try not to spoil this hap-py new year.

Dandelion

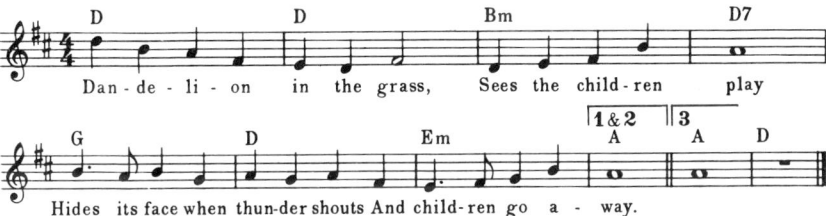

Dan-de-li-on in the grass, Sees the child-ren play Hides its face when thun-der shouts And child-ren go a - way.

It's a Rainy Day

1 Shi - ny pave-ment on the ground, Each lor - ry makes a swish-ing sound.
2 Old boots now look wet and new, My coat is chang-ing col - our too, And

Wa - ter plants splash in the street, And pud - dles part be - neath my
in the park the dust has gone, The plants have got their jew - els

vv. 1 & 4 (after v. 4 to Coda ⊕)

feet; It's a rain-y day.
on; It's a rain-y day.

v. 2 only

3 Catch - ing rain-drops on my tongue Is tast-ing where the

clouds come from, I clean my knees by running fast In all the long-est

wet - mop grass On a rain-y day.

From 𝄋 for verse 4:

When it stops the fun is gone
Although the wetness lingers on.
But puddles give a sudden peep
Into a world beneath my feet,
On a rainy day.

CODA

5 Rain - - y day, Sounds of sum-mer in the

rain. Come and play. It's a rain-y day.

Slubberdegullion's Song

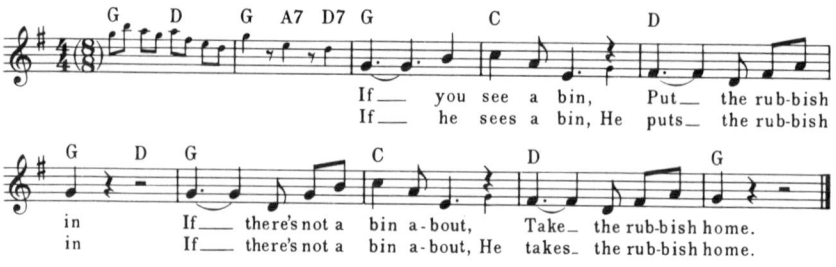

If__ you see a bin, Put__ the rub-bish
If__ he sees a bin, He puts__ the rub-bish

in If__ there's not a bin a-bout, Take__ the rub-bish home.
in If__ there's not a bin a-bout, He takes__ the rub-bish home.

The Shepherd and His Dog

They be climb-ing up the hill, All our sheep, all our sheep; For the

morn-ing air be chill, And the fields they lie still, And the

wor-dle be a - sleep, Say the Shep-herd and his dog.____

David's Shepherd's Song

The sheep on the hill-side And sheep by the stream Are

peace-ful-ly graz-ing where bright wa-ters gleam. But sheep in the val-ley are

trem-bling with fright Sur-round-ed by wolves in the dark-ness of night.

108

The Little Drummer Boy

Come, they told me, pa - rum pum pum pum ___ A new-born king to see, pa - rum pum pum pum ___ Our fin-est gifts we bring, pa - rum pum pum pum ___ To lay be - fore the king, pa - rum pum pum pum, rum pum pum pum rum pum pum pum ___ So to hon-our him, pa - rum pum pum pum ___ When we come. ___

The Cherry Tree Carol

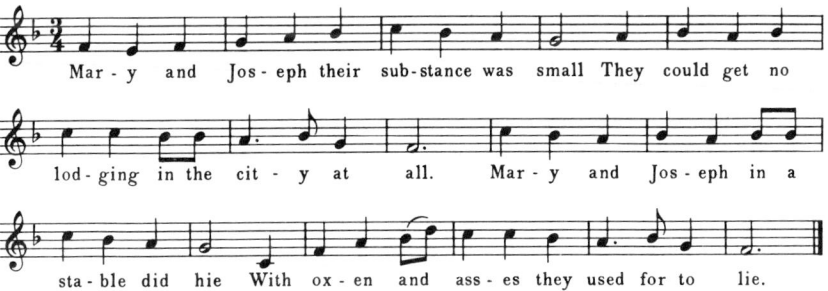

Mar - y and Jos - eph their sub-stance was small They could get no lod - ging in the cit - y at all. Mar - y and Jos - eph in a sta - ble did hie With ox - en and ass - es they used for to lie.

Baboushka's Carol

Acknowledgments

Acknowledgment is due to the following:

William Collins Sons and Company, Limited for *The Star of the Nativity* by Boris Pasternak translated by Max Hayward and Manya Harari contained in *Dr Zhivago* (Epilogue)].

Chappell Music Limited for *The Little Drummer Boy.*
Words and Music by Harry Simeone, Henry Onorati and Katherine K. Davis, © 1958 Mills Music Inc. and Delaware Music Corp. By arrangement with Shawnee Press Inc. Assigned 1963 to International Korwin Corp.

Routledge and Kegan Paul Limited for *The Shepherd and His Dog,* (by an old shepherd) from *The Chime Child or Somerset Singers,* edited by Ruth Tongue.

Russell and Volkening Inc. as agents for the author, for *Hello's a Handy Word* from *Nuts to You and Nuts to Me,* © 1974 by Mary Ann Hoberman.

Mirror Group Newspapers for *Anger* by Yvonne Low from *Junior Voices Book 1* published Penguin Books Ltd.

The musical accompaniments to *Hello's a Handy Word, Talking, It's a Rainy Day, Slubberdegullion* and *Baboushka's Carol* were written by Peter Hutchings, those to *It's Not Much Fun, Dandelion, Blackbird's Song* and *David's Shepherd's Song* by Albert Chatterley, and those to *New Things To Do* and *The Cherry Tree Carol* by Pamela Kenway (used by permission).

The editor would like to thank the consultants for the series, Gwen Dunn and Patricia Wilkinson, the staff and children of Summercroft Infants School for helping to choose the stories, and the designer of this book, Helen Howie.